NOSTALGIA SPOTLIGHT ON THE THIRTIES

Michael Anglo

First published in 1976 by
JUPITER BOOKS(LONDON) LIMITED
167 Hermitage Road, London N4 1LZ.

Copyright © Jupiter Books (London) Limited 1976

SBN 904041 484

This edition produced in 1985 by
Universal Books Ltd.,
The Grange,
Grange Yard,
London SE1 3AG

41448

Composed on the Monotype in 12/14pt Baskerville 169 by

HBM Typesetting Limited, Chorley, Lancashire.

Printed and Bound by R. J. Acford, Chichester.

Contents

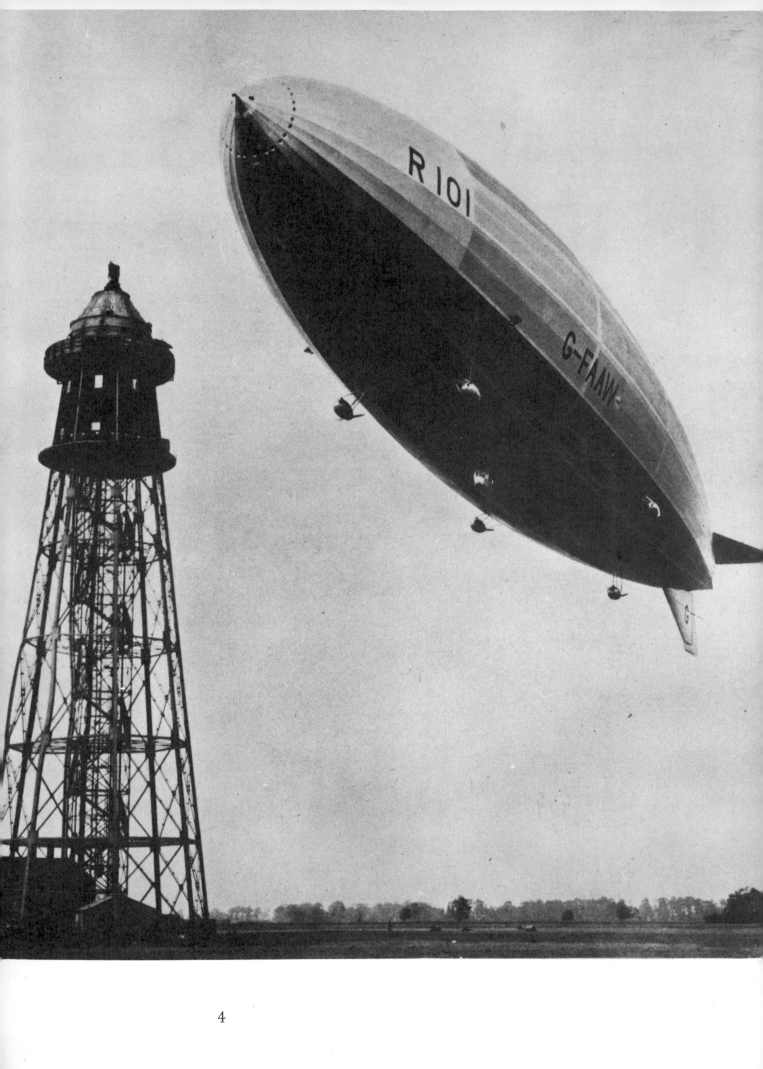

The grey white elephants

O N THE NIGHT OF 5 OCTOBER, 1930 THE ROAR OF WHAT sounded like a squadron of aeroplanes flying directly overhead brought us running into the backyard. The weather was damp and blustery as we saw flying low over the rooftops the airship *R101*, starting its ill-fated maiden voyage, a flight to India. News of the preparations for the flight had been occupying columns in the newspapers for months and like most boys at the time I was interested in all aircraft, particularly in the airship. That very afternoon I had been to the cinema to see *Flight*, an air picture starring Jack Holt.

I watched the great airship for a moment or two through the naked branches of our lone tree, a sycamore. The cabins and gondolas were lighted and the black silhouette of the fat cigar-shaped airship seemed to be sailing dangerously low. Furthermore, it seemed to be yawing badly, moving slowly almost crabwise beneath billowing bundles of ominous dirty cloud.

My mother often talked about Zeppelin raids on London that had taken place during World War One and how she had seen a Zeppelin shot down in flames over Potters Bar. At the Imperial War Museum I had actually seen a Zeppelin observation car which had been cut loose from a German raider. I had even visited sites in London as far apart as Stratford and Long Acre where bombs had fallen.

I also have vague memories of seeing an airship flying over London when I was a child. My mother told me that it had been the *R34* starting on its flight to America. But my impressions of that last look at the *R101* are vivid.

That night I dreamt I was standing on the Eiffel Tower in Paris when, approaching in the distance, I saw the *R101*. Suddenly it dipped, crashed into a hillside and burst into flames. The next morning I came downstairs to get the Sunday newspapers from the letterbox and there it was, all over the front pages. The airship had indeed crashed into a hillside near Beauvais, not far from Paris, at two o'clock that morning, killing forty-six of the fifty-four passengers aboard. The fact that I had had such a vivid dream about the disaster made me almost believe for a while that I had somehow become endowed with superhuman powers, but it seemed I had not been the only one to dream about the

The *R101* made her trial flight in October 1929 and flew over London during an air display in June 1930.

5

crash. Many people wrote to the newspapers about having had similar dreams.

Of course there had been nothing clairvoyant about my dream. The fact that I had always been fascinated by aircraft, had seen a film featuring air crashes the previous afternoon, had read enough about aircraft to realise that the *R101* had not seemed to be flying properly and had even visualised it crashing, and had read about the course the airship was taking on its flight to India, were enough to induce the dream of the fatal crash. Even the Eiffel Tower could be explained as I had often thought of it as a suitable mooring mast for an airship.

During the days that followed, there were many photographs in the newspapers of the dead, the few survivors, and the twisted wreckage reminiscent of the photographs I had seen of Zeppelins shot down in the Great War. For many months echoes of the disaster appeared in newspapers and magazines providing more material for my scrapbook.

In July 1932 I was seated in the front cockpit of an Avro 504K trainer aircraft flying over the sea outside Brighton. The pilot, a friend of a cousin with whom I was staying, banked the plane steeply toward the airfield at Shoreham and, glancing back, I was amazed to see a huge shape looming low over the sea. I turned to the pilot and pointed. He grinned and nodded. He had already seen it. It was a gigantic air-ship. The pilot banked the plane again and flew out to sea away from the airship then made an Immelmann turn to come in above and behind it. I squeezed the trigger of my imaginary twin machine guns and sent a long burst of tracer tearing into the hide of the monster. He banked away again then turned back to fly parallel with the airship. I could read the name *Graf Zeppelin* painted on its side. I swung my guns on the scarff mounting and put in another quick burst. I could see the Germans in the gondolas and they seemed to be waving. We did not wave back and veered away. I think I was disappointed that I had failed to emulate Leefe-Robinson.

The most famous airship of all times was undoubtedly the *Graf Zeppelin*. Laid down as the LZ127 in 1927, the airship was launched the following year and immediately Dr Hugo Eckener, head of the Zeppelin works and veteran commander, proceeded to set about the task of re-establishing the reputation of the airship as a means of transport. By the beginning of the next decade the German airship had made flights to the U.S.A., cruises to the Arctic and the tropics and a round-the-world cruise in 1929, safely weathering storms and typhoons and averaging a flying speed of 70 m.p.h.

The *Graf Zeppelin* had a main sitting room, two smaller saloons and cabins with berths for twenty-four passengers, all on one deck. The leisurely speed of the aircraft and the low altitude at which it flew, often

The *R101* in her early glory
and *below* wrecked on
Beauvais Ridge.

7

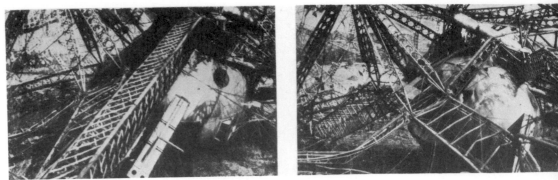

Dr Eckener, commander of
the *Graf Zeppelin*.

less than the length of the airship itself, enabled the passengers to see practically every detail of the country over which the airship passed.

In 1930 the airship flew to South America via the Cape Verde Islands where it dropped sacks of mail by parachute. Among the passengers were Prince Alfonso of Spain and the famous news correspondent and inveterate traveller, Lady Drummond Hay. Later that year the Zeppelin flew to Moscow on what was hopefully called a goodwill mission to promote aviation intercourse between Germany and Russia. Naturally, where the *Graf Zeppelin* flew it engendered a vast amount of publicity and curiosity and it was ever the shining example to airship designers in both Britain and America who were battling unsuccessfully to produce viable airships of their own. Meanwhile the Germans capitalised on their superiority in this area and publicised into heroes Zeppelin commanders Eckener and Lehman who were soon known throughout the world.

The Zeppelin flew a twenty-four hour circuit of Britain in August 1931 with a party of aerial trippers who paid £30 per head for the privilege. Representatives of the British upper crust were prominent among the passenger list which included Colonel the Master of Sempill, Lieutenant-Colonel Shelmondine, Director of Civil Aviation, the Countess of Drogheda, Lord Inverclyde and Lady Warborough.

The route taken by the airship was from Hanworth to the Sussex coast, the Isle of Wight, Exeter, Teignmouth, across to Wexford, Waterford, Dublin, Belfast, Glasgow, Edinburgh and back down the east coast to London. The newspapers reported that scenes of tumultuous welcome marked the arrival of the airship at Hanworth where she was greeted by the broadcast strains of 'Deutschland Uber Alles'. It was twelve years after World War One and eight years before World War Two.

Almost a year later the *Graf Zeppelin* was back again in Britain flying leisurely over London on its way to Hanworth from Friedrichshafen. A few passengers disembarked, a party of twenty-four boarded and it made another cruise over the island. No doubt the crew's cameras were clicking busily, taking useful pictures for later reference.

By November 1932 the Zeppelin had made two hundred and ninety voyages totalling some 330,000 miles; it had carried 17,000 passengers,

The *Graf Zeppelin* at
Hanworth Park in July 1932.

40,000 lb. of mail and 80,000 lb. of freight, but not until 21 March 1932 did it begin a regularly scheduled transoceanic service averaging twenty-two passengers for each cruise. The cost per head was £142 – a not inconsiderable sum in those days.

The food and service in the dining room aboard the airship were reputed to equal the first class standards of transatlantic passenger liners with almost as much comfort. By the beginning of 1935 the *Graf Zeppelin* had made ninety ocean crossings, carried 27,000 passengers, five and a half million postal packets and over forty tons of freight, without mishap.

But of course, travelling on the *Graf Zeppelin* was not always as comfortable as it was cracked up to be. On the first world cruise there had been no heating and the passengers were nearly frozen flying over Siberia. Washing facilities had been limited and the passengers washed in rotation in small metal hand basins and there was often a shortage of water. One passenger remarked that the tiny electric kitchen range had been hardly adequate for haute cuisine.

The *Graf Zeppelin* flew on and on throughout the thirties covering a total of more than a million miles before being taken out of service

9

when the newly built Zeppelin, the *Hindenburg*, came to its tragic end in 1937.

In 1919 the British airship *R34* had made the first successful airship crossings of the Atlantic, flying from Britain to the U.S.A. and back again in ten days. Eleven years later the *R100*, whose construction had been backed by industry in virtual competition with the *R101* built by the government, left the airship base at Cardington to fly to Montreal, Canada. Despite several spells of extremely rough weather and damage caused to a fin in high winds, a record trip was made. Repairs to the fin were made en route and subsequent damage to an engine during landing at Montreal were dismissed lightly. The airship actually returned home flying on five engines.

Despite the miserable series of setbacks, mishaps and disasters that bedevilled airship development during this period, experts were still full of enthusiasm about the future of airship travel. The *R38*, built in Britain and sold to the United States government, had broken her back in the air near Hull in 1921 with a loss of forty-four lives. In 1923 a

The *Graf Zeppelin* at Hanworth on its first round-Britain tour in August 1931.

German Zeppelin taken over by the French government and renamed the *Dixmude*, was blown out to sea and lost with thirty hands aboard. In 1925 the U.S. lost the *Shenandoah* with fourteen of its crew. But nobody was yet ready to give up the struggle to establish the airship as queen of the air.

The *R100* took three days to make its return journey from Montreal to Cardington, and one of the passengers describing the journey claimed that a glass of water placed on a table in a cabin when he left Montreal was unspilled when he arrived at Cardington; the tall vases of flowers on the tables in the dining room had also remained undisturbed. He said that if it were possible he would never travel on a surface ship again and that he sought to book a passage to India on the *R101*. The *R101* crashed in flames a few months later.

The passenger cabins on the *R100* had white linen walls and ceilings. There was a large dining room and a lounge with a kitchen at one end, lined on two sides by curtained cabins. On the balcony above were more cabins and at the back was the crew's living room with cabins opening off it. The cabins had two berths, one above the other, each

Britons greet the *Zeppelin*.

The *Graf Zeppelin* visiting
Moscow in September 1930,
and over the Arctic.

Above, Lord Thompson.
Below, Sir Sefton Brancker.

with a laced canvas on which a sleeping bag was placed. There was a communal washroom. Baggage allowance for each passenger was thirty pounds.

The *R101* built by the British government had been designed by almost the same team which had built the ill-fated *R38*. The great new airship, captained by Flight Lieutenant H. C. Irwin A.F.C., left its base at Cardington at 7.36 p.m. on 4 October 1930 to fly to India. Passengers included Lord Thompson, Minister for Air; Air Vice Marshal Sir Sefton Brancker, Director of Civil Aviation; and Wing Commander Colmore, Director of Airship Development.

At 9.21 p.m. the *R101* passed over London and was seen by thousands of people. It crossed the English coast at 10.47 p.m. at an altitude of just seven hundred feet; it reached the French coast at 12.36 a.m. and less than two hours later was seen over Beauvais losing height. A little later it crashed into a hillside at Allonne and burst into flames.

The start of the flight from Cardington had been marked by the sluggishness of one of the engines and later by the casting overboard of ballast comprising twenty-five tons of fuel oil and eight tons of water. The hydrogen-filled ship had run into a storm while crossing the Channel; wind and rain lashed the airship, soaking the gigantic envelope and weighing it down. The cumbersome craft flew low over the French countryside in continuing bad weather. Finally, the impact when it struck the hill was followed by an explosion and conflagration which left only a skeleton of girders, but neatly positioned in a manner which suggested that had the ship been filled with non-inflammable helium instead of hydrogen, there might have been many more surviviors. But the cost of helium was more than twenty times that of hydrogen.

At the inquiry into the disaster, faults in the design of the *R101* were found and it was revealed that bracing wires had been chafing the gasbags as long ago as a year before; that a cable controlling an elevator was found to have been broken prior to the accident and that an altimeter had been faulty. Leakage of gas, and sparks from a broken electrical circuit had been responsible for the fire. With the crash of the *R101* crashed all Britain's aspirations in the field of airship development.

The Americans had been experimenting with naval airships throughout the twenties. The *Los Angeles*, built for America by the Germans as part of war reparations, was flown across to America by Hugo Eckener. Making its debut in 1924, it made two hundred and fifty subsequent flights, including trips to Panama and Puerto Rico before it was decommissioned in 1932.

At Akron, Ohio, in 1931, the Americans completed a vast airship, 785 feet in length, which was christened, naturally enough, the *Akron*. Armed with heavy machine guns and no external gondolas it presented a formidable appearance like some gigantic torpedo, but in 1933 the

13

The naval airship *Akron*, which carried five aircraft inside its hull.

million dollar naval airship was wrecked in a storm off the coast of New Jersey with the loss of seventy-three crewmen. The *Macon*, a sister ship to the *Akron*, was completed in 1933. It crashed off the coast of California in 1935. Fortunately seventy-three of the seventy-six crew survived the accident. After this tragedy the U.S. decided to make no more dirigibles, although many smaller airships of non-rigid design continued to fly.

But the German *Graf Zeppelin* was still going strong and construction by Germany of a new larger Zeppelin, designated the *L129*, was well under way. In 1936 the strongly-built ship was launched and named the *Hindenburg*. This was the airship to supersede the *Graf Zeppelin* on the North Atlantic run. The biggest airship ever to fly, it was over eight hundred feet long and had four motor gondolas, each supporting a sixteen cylinder Daimler-Benz diesel motor.

The airship carried a new type of altimeter which emitted a shrill whistle, the echo of which bounced from the surface of the land or sea

The *Akron* over New York and
right, the *Akron's* remains,
recovered from the sea.

16

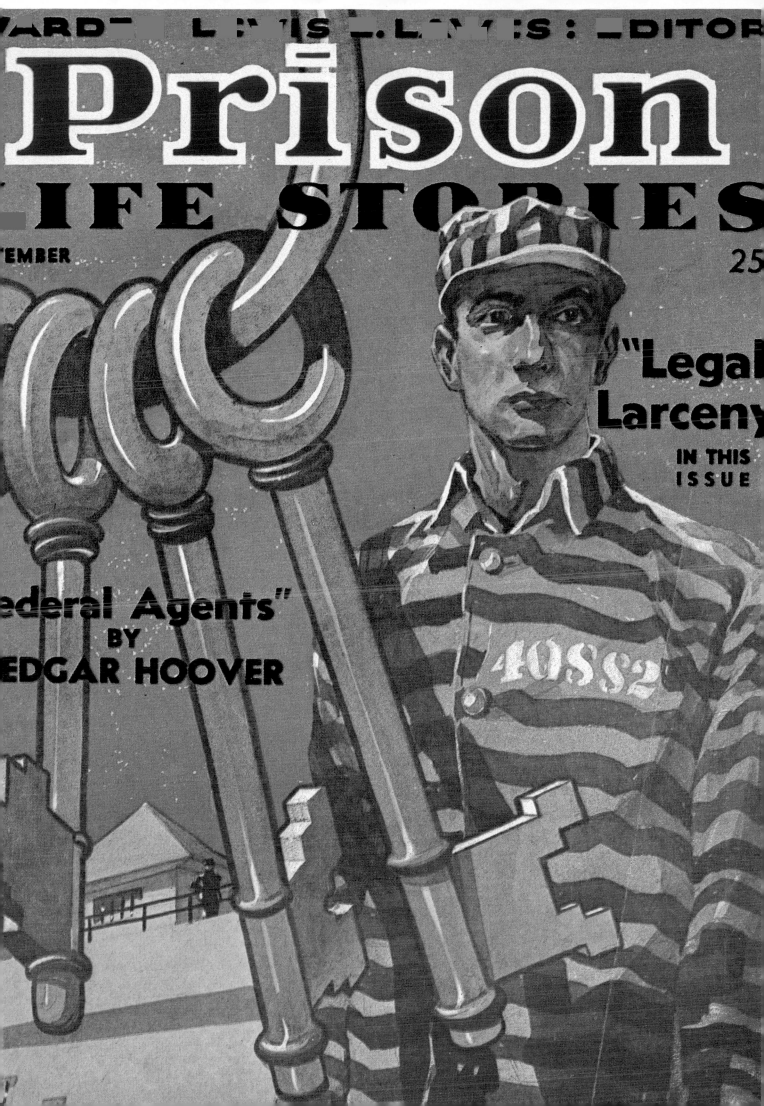

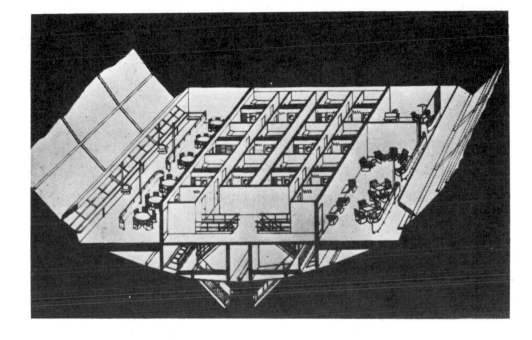

over which the airship was passing and recorded the altitude in metres
on a dial in the navigating room. It was claimed that this and other
improved instruments would make it possible to land the airship on the
blackest night or in thick fog. The ship carried the most powerful
electrical plant ever built into an aircraft. A further addition for night
flying was a five and a half million candle power searchlight which
enabled the navigator to use the drift meter by night as well as by day.
The lower deck of the airship contained an all-electric kitchen, the
crew's mess and a smoking room which could seat twenty-five people
with room for many more standing to take the view from the sloping
windows. A stairway like the gangway of a ship led up to another deck
where there were twenty-five two-berth cabins. All inside rooms were
equipped with hot and cold running water, a curtained wardrobe,
additional hooks for clothes, a service bell and ventilation control. On
one side of these cabins was the dining saloon, with a general saloon and
reading and writing room on the other. Railed off around the rooms
was a low promenade. All these amenities occupied floor space four
times that of the *Graf Zeppelin*.

On 6 May 1937, as the *Hindenburg* was approaching the moorings at
New Jersey, U.S.A., with just a few more yards to go, there was a
sudden burst of terrifying flame from the tail of the ship which spread
rapidly forward, engulfing the whole envelope. Within seconds, before
a crowd of horrified spectators, the massive ship was reduced to a
twisted wreck of blackened girders and metal piping. Yet, miracu-
lously, sixty-two of the ninety-seven people on board survived the
holocaust.

The shocked Germans immediately took the *Graf Zeppelin* out of
service but a sister ship of the *Hindenburg* was completed with the hope

that the U.S.A. would supply non-inflammable helium. Some hopes! The U.S.A. refused to consider supplying what was thought to be such an invaluable asset, especially as German military ambitions were being viewed with increasing alarm. So further development of the dirigible was doomed.

Static electricity was blamed for the last disaster though it was also suggested that the ship had been sabotaged. Nevertheless, the new airship, also named the *Graf Zeppelin*, was used to spy along the British coast until August 1939, one month before the outbreak of war, when the Germans took it out of service.

The observation trapdoor on top of the *R100*.

The last *Graf Zeppelin*.

Talkie time

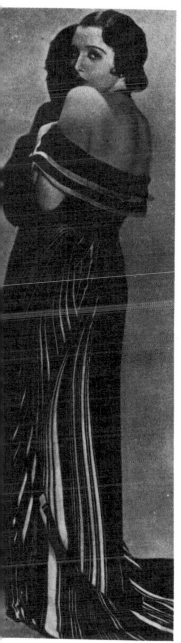

Bebe Daniels.

UNTIL RECENTLY I HAD ALWAYS BEEN A MOVIE FAN AND as far as films are concerned I have a long-ranging memory, but I was not very impressed by the first talkies. I did not like the way the stars, at the slightest provocation or, for that matter, without any provocation whatsoever, were liable to break into sudden song without any relevance to the story. I tried to avoid going to see musicals, but that was not always possible as my mother liked them and I had to sit and suffer through quite a few. I did manage not to see Al Jolson sing 'Sonny Boy' in *The Jazz Singer*. Even now, I must confess, I am not very fond of the human voice in song, be it bursting in opera or popping in pop. However I was to have my day with the talkies. Films like *Hell's Angels* and *All Quiet on the Western Front* were more my cup of tea and soon I was having quite a tea party as more and more films were becoming less song ridden.

I certainly had my favourites among the stars of the thirties – James Cagney, Lloyd Nolan, Jack Holt, Wallace Beery and Buster Keaton. It was not until I was about sixteen that I began to take notice of female stars, but I would never go to the cinema especially to see one although, when I think about it, I must admit that I did find Jean Harlow, Anne Sothern and Myrna Loy attractive.

Hell's Angels, a film which featured spectacular scenes of aerial combat in World War One, was very much to my liking and I saw it three times. During the last war, Ben Lyon, star of *Hell's Angels*, appeared in a very successful radio series with his famous Hollywood movie star wife, Bebe Daniels, and they often made references to the film and his heroic role in it, as a sort of a running joke. I have often wondered why the movie has never been brought to the TV screen. Older and far worse movies have been resuscitated and foisted onto a hapless public.

Erich Remarque's *All Quiet on the Western Front* was shown on television and I saw it for my third time. Lew Ayres, the young star who played Paul Baumer, went on to star in the immensely popular series of 'Dr. Kildare' films with Lionel Barrymore.

As a schoolboy I sneaked off with a school chum from a London

19

exhibition of French art around which our form was being conducted, to go to the Tivoli in the Strand to see Boris Karloff in *Frankenstein*. Little did I realise that I was in at the start of a film fashion which was to last, it now seems, forever. My friend and I found the film more funny than frightening but not quite as funny as Bela Lugosi in *Dracula* which I saw later. I do not think I missed many of the gangster films that streamed in steadily from Hollywood in the late twenties and thirties. I remember particularly Wallace Beery in *The Secret Six*, Paul Muni in *Scarface* and James Cagney in *G-Men*. Edward G. Robinson comes to my mind playing his first role as Charlie Young, a Chinese

20

Hell's Angels. Top, Zeppelin gunners in action. *Above,* Germans dumping spares in an attempt to elude British fighters. *Right,* a German Gotha used in the film.

21

gangster in a movie about the tong wars and hatchet men in America. I think Robinson's catchphrase in the movie was, 'Charlie Young, wise guy; wise guy, Charlie Young. Fifty-fifty Chinaman,' . . . and of course, the term 'hatchet man', a sort of Chinese hitman whose weapon was an axe, came into general usage.

There were several films about the French Foreign Legion. I went to see, among them, *Beau Geste*, starring Ronald Colman, and *Beau Ideal*. One film I saw with a girlfriend was *The Great Ziegfield*, a super musical starring William Powell. It seemed to last for ever and I hated every minute of it. As for westerns in the thirties, I would take them or leave them alone. I hankered after the cowboy films of my earlier days. Nobody could replace Tom Mix, Hoot Gibson, Buck Jones and Jack Hoxie. I saw Joel McCrea and Frances Dee in *Wells Fargo*. The movie was about the days when the pony express was giving way to communication by rail and telegraph and I was sorry it ever happened. As I remember it, as the pace of communication increased in the movie, the pace of the movie itself decreased.

I think the last western I saw before the war broke out was *Stagecoach*, in which John Wayne rode into pictures. It has since been shown on television and was worth a laugh. They do not make westerns like that anymore. Thank the Lord.

Nowadays, I do not go to the cinema unless I have to because of my work, although I do like Paul Newman. In fact, the last time I went to the movies on my own initiative was a few years ago to see Paul Newman in *The Towering Inferno*. I wait for the movies to come round on TV. By that time when they are chopped down to size, it is easier to see the big holes and tatty corners in a lot of them and I can congratulate myself for not having wasted money at the cinema. Anyway, I think cinemas today are claustrophobic with no ambiance, none of the grand atmosphere of old and the films themselves are not good enough reason for me to get up, go out, and as likely as not finish up with a nasty taste in my mouth. Or perhaps now that I am older and jaded I have outgrown the cinema. Or perhaps after years of cinema-going the gilt really is off the gingerbread. Come back Milton Sills and Nazimova! All is forgiven.

At the beginning of the thirties, people were already turning away from the stereotyped musical being churned out by most of the motion picture studios. Stories were trivial and just a medium for songs and music. Having had a surfeit of this sort of pap, the public was demanding a little change in the diet. The novelty of the sound movie had worn off. Sound for the sake of it was just not good enough. That is not to say that talkies like *Gold Diggers of Broadway* and *Love Parade* were not a success. But fresh items were wanted in the weekly movie meal: films

with a story, films with a message, films with realism, films made on location, stars who could talk and act, not just sing songs. And such films were made. *Hell's Angels* was spectacle drama with the immortal Jean Harlow. *All Quiet on the Western Front* was a brilliant anti-war film. Cedric Hardwicke's *The Dreyfus Case* had a message about anti-Semitism, a message which unfortunately, so many people did not seem to get. *The Blue Angel* at the London Dominion in 1930 launched Marlene Dietrich through the next five decades.

In 1931 Charlie Chaplin made *City Lights* and Gloria Swanson *The Widow and the Law*. In Hollywood, Dorothy de Barba, a child prodigy, was signed up for a phenomenal salary of £100 a week; Shirley Temple had not yet arrived. Another child prodigy, said to be the new Jackie Coogan, was Peter Lawford, aged seven. The press was lauding what they called the spectacular rise of the British film industry to become second only to Hollywood in importance. Its main centre was at Elstree in the studios of British International Pictures Limited. Important films were also being made in Germany and France, and even Norway was producing all-Norwegian films such as *The Daughter of the North*, a story about Lapland. But unquestionably Hollywood continued to dominate the movie market.

After the 'smash hits' *The Singing Fool* and *The Jazz Singer*, Al Jolson made *Mammy* with Louis Moran and Lowell Sherman in which he continued his tear jerking songs. In 1932, the Gaumont company produced *Rome Express* at Shepherds Bush Studios, London. Directed by Walter Forde, the film, starring the blooming blonde Esther Ralston, was shot entirely in the studios. The Paris terminus, the Gare de Lyon, the French style locomotive and carriages were all constructed on the set.

Stars such as Claudette Colbert, Clive Brook, Genevieve Tobin,

Grand Hotel. Right, Greta Garbo. *Below,* Joan Crawford and Wallace Beery.

Above, Virginia Bruce.
Right, Charlie Chaplin and
Virginia Cherrill in *City
Lights*.

26

Above, Chaplin arriving in Britain in 1931. *Top right*, Joan Bennett, who played opposite George Arliss in *Disraeli*.
Right, Miriam Hopkins in *The World and the Flesh*. *Lower right*, Herbert Marshall, Norma Shearer and Clark Gable in 1934.

Ann Sothern.

Basil Rathbone, and Jessie Matthews all appeared in films in 1932 and that was the year that Alexander Korda discovered Diana Napier and Merle Oberon. Charles Laughton appeared as a submarine captain in *The Devil and the Deep*, with Tallulah Bankhead as his wife and Gary Cooper as his lieutenant. The critics were not too kind about the film. It was said that although Tallulah in her role was faultless, and Cooper heroic, Laughton was unconvincing and that his casting had been unfortunate. The story, grim and somewhat crude, was about the captain's insane jealousy over his wife's relationship with the dour lieutenant, causing him deliberately to wreck his submarine and perish in the disaster.

The critics granted that Laughton in his mad moments was terrifying, but saw no point in a naval setting to so hoary a story. One critic wrote that although he had never visited a submarine base in a remote part of the African coast, he would be willing to bet a coconut to a peanut that Paris gowns and antique furniture were unlikely to be found in such a setting.

In September 1932 a film about Hindenburg's victorious battle

28

Right, Sylvia Sidney as an Apache girl in *Behold My Wife*. *Below*, Gary Cooper, Charles Laughton and Tallulah Bankhead in *The Devil and the Deep* in 1932. *Right*, there were chimpanzees acting in the film *Little Covered Wagons* years before the tea monkeys of television.

against the Russians at Tannenburg in World War One was made by Herr Heinz Paul, the German film producer. Realism, if not truth, was a feature of German films of the period and this film for German consumption was not of the same mould as *All Quiet on the Western Front*, which had been banned in Germany. Nero was quick off the mark with another German production, *M* which was about the Düsseldorf vampire. Peter Kürten, the real Düsseldorf vampire, had only been executed in 1931. (For a full discussion, see the previous book in this series.)

Vicki Baum's masterpiece, *Grand Hotel*, was made by M.G.M. and had a scintillating cast. Garbo played the passé prima ballerina Grasinskaya although she looked anything but passé, Wallace Beery played the director, Preysing, and Joan Crawford was Flaemmchen, the secretary whom Preysing proposed to take to England with him. Lionel Barrymore and Lewis Stone were also in the cast.

An American film called *College Humour*, a Hollywood version of contemporary university life was panned by English critics who decried the use of 'crooning', the popular singing style of the period, in a film. It was about rivalry between Richard Arlen, a football star, and Jack Oakie, a crooner who, said the critics, had been given a series of excruciatingly unfunny remarks by the screenwriters which belied the title. The British film public, who patronised the local cinemas, did not seem to agree with the critics.

In August 1933 *King Kong* arrived in England, to become a movie institution. Sitting astride the top of the Empire State Building in New

Fay Wray in 1935.

York, clutching Fay Wray in one hand and swatting fighter planes with the other the ill-used monster won a place in everyone's heart. Diana Wynyard and Clive Brook starred in the spectacular *Cavalcade* which about this time was proving a great attraction to American moviegoers curious about the British Empire and all that. News of Hollywood and picture people was eagerly lapped up by movie fans all over the world and publicity pedlars were using soft brushes to tone down the lurid pictures they had previously painted of Hollywood in the pre-depression days. Now they gave idyllic accounts of how quietly the stars were living with just a mansion or two and the odd swimming pool in Beverly Hills, and the little old beach bungalow simply furnished, a few custom built cars and suchlike. When not working they were leading an almost English country existence: tennis parties, tea, crumpets and home made cakes and small dinner parties for no more than eight people with bridge or friendly chat to follow. Some played golf at the Lakeside club or, 'in a burst of gaiety', visited the Coconut Grove dance restaurant at the Ambassadors Hotel in Los Angeles. Of course, it was pointed out, there was glamour in Hollywood, for one might pass Lupe Velez in her giant car speeding down some palm-lined boulevard or meet Jean Harlow or Elizabeth Allan doing their morning shopping at some open air fruit market; or in a health club find Edmund Lowe having a Turkish bath or Johnny Weissmuller playing squash. It all helped to brighten the lives of millions who never had a snowball's chance in hell of doing the Hollywood rubbing of shoulders bit.

31

Robert Donat as Culpepper and Franklyn Dyall as Cromwell in *The Private Life of Henry VIII*.

Dinner at Eight was advertised as the picture of the year in 1933. In this adaptation of the Kaufman-Ferber play, Jean Harlow played Kitty Packard, pampered wife of a selfmade man. However, the film that made a lasting impact that year was undoubtedly *The Private Life of Henry VIII*. Charles Laughton gave one of the finest performances of his career in the part of the king, presenting the bluff, jovial side of the randy king's character rather than his selfishness, viciousness, cruelty and downright unsavoury mien. Merle Oberon played Anne Boleyn, maid of honour to Catherine of Aragon, who attracted the lascivious attentions of Henry. Robert Donat played Culpepper, lover of Catherine Howard. Thomas Dyall took the part of Thomas Cromwell, unscrupulous successor of the disgraced Wolsey who, to further his own political ends, devised the marriage of Henry and the unlovely Anne of Cleves played by Elsa Lanchester. A big feature of the film was the claim that it twisted history 'only a bit' and the public was 'spared any sign of bad taste', not the sort of claim that would particularly recommend a film today.

Morning Glory opened at the London Coliseum in November 1933 and Katharine Hepburn as a stage struck girl was hailed as a star of the first magnitude. The story of the film was said to resemble that of Hepburn's life in many details. In the film, a girl with high ambitions,

BOYS' COMICS OF THE THIRTIES
Top left: Hotspur, 1935.
Top right: Modern Boy, August 1939.
Lower right: The Champion, 1938.

Cinema advertisement slides of the early 1930s. These simple hand-painted glass slides were placed in a projector and afforded a cheap means of reaching the captive cinema audiences.

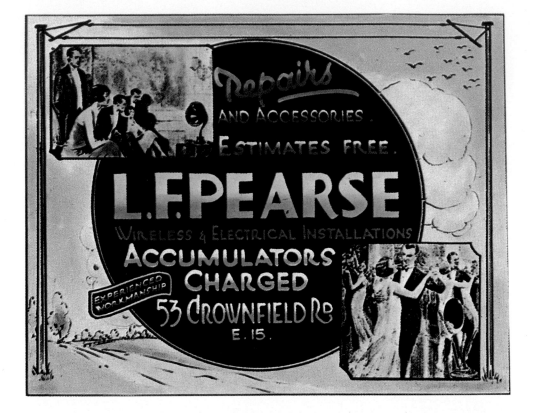

Charles Laughton as the king, *right,* and *below,* a banquet scene from the film.

33

Berkeley Square. Right, Valerie Taylor. *Far right,* Heather Angel and Leslie Howard.

she sought the advice of a veteran actor played by the veteran actor C. Aubrey Smith. Adolf Menjou was the big time stage producer and the young struggling writer was Douglas Fairbanks Jr. looking very junior in those days.

White Woman, a Paramount picture of life in the Malayan jungle starred Carole Lombard and Charles Laughton, and Leslie Howard starred in the Fox film, *Berkeley Square*, an adaptation from the play. Howard played the role of a young man who returned to the past and lived the life of one of his ancestors.

The Wall Street slump followed by the depression had hit Hollywood hard and the effects lasted for a long while. It was said that Wallace Beery, a heavy investor in the stock market, had lost a fortune, and Eddie Cantor who had amassed two million dollars was left with bundles of worthless share certificates. Al Jolson had three million dollars invested in the market and lost the lot. Cinema receipts had fallen and Hollywood cut first its production, then salaries. But a good deal of the publicised economies was studio ballyhoo and the publicity boys churned out their apocryphal anecdotes for a commiserating public who could identify with the plight of the stars.

Newspapers, magazines and radios announced the shattering news. Gary Cooper had walked all around Hollywood trying to change a one

Top, Fred Astaire in 1935.
Top right, Ginger Rogers.
Above, Joel McCrea in Wells
Fargo.

hundred dollar bill; Frederic March opened the money-box of his adopted son and took enough ready money to carry on until the banks opened again. Wallace Beery switched off the electric lights in his mansion and used only candles and sold his limousine; his wife began to make her own dresses. Movie fans were heartbroken.

Then the harassed stars received another devastating blow. Under Roosevelt's National Recovery Act, it was declared that no star should receive a salary of more than two thousand dollars a week, not an inconsiderable salary at that, but the stars howled blue murder as they are apt to do at the mere mention of income tax nowadays. They soon got together to argue whether the act was legally justifiable. All the same, boy star Jackie Cooper still earned more than President Roosevelt, and Mae West would have felt down in the dumps more than somewhat if she had entered the White House.

At the beginning of 1934 the London Film Company followed the success of their *Private Life of Henry VIII* with Elizabeth Bergner playing the title role of *Catherine the Great* and Korda popped up with Douglas Fairbanks and Merle Oberon in *The Private Life of Don Juan* made at Elstree, to perpetuate the 'Private Life' theme. Noel Coward appeared playing the part of a publisher in one of his first films, *The Scoundrel*, and Cedric Hardwicke as the Marquess of Steyne, starred in *Becky Sharp*,

35

the first full length colour film at the New Gallery with Frances Dee playing Amelia Selby. *Natasha*, the London Film production about Czarist Russia, starred Laurence Olivier as Ignaloff, and a documentary called *B.B.C., the Voice of Britain*, offering a peep behind the scenes at Broadcasting House, was shown at the Carlton Theatre. Of this jejune production, a well known contemporary critic wrote bitingly, 'Since this film has been made by the Post Office Film Unit one cannot, of course, expect the peep to reveal things in an unfavourable light. If the motto might well be "see how wonderful we all are!" this is a profitable piece of back-scratching on the whole. Sir John Reith himself is not seen; a similar sort of inhibition exists, I believe, in the matter of representing the Divinity and the Royal Family on either screen or stage.'

Sir John Reith, head of the B.B.C. in those days, often came in for plenty of fiery criticism, but he was fireproof.

James Cagney, always a great favourite with the British public had appeared in many movies including *Mayor of Hell* with Frankie Darro. In 1934, in a Cosmopolitan picture, *Devil Dogs of the Air*, at the Regal Cinema, Marble Arch, Cagney played Jefferson O'Toole. The film was a Hollywood version of life in a U.S. marine air training school. Cagney also starred with Olivia de Havilland in Warner Brothers' *The Irish in Us*.

In September 1934 the British Dominion film, *Peg of Old Drury*, opened at the Leicester Square Theatre. The film had as its theme the love story of the great actor David Garrick and Margaret Woffington,

Barbara Stanwyck in *Shopworn* in 1932.

36

his famous partner. Cedric Hardwicke was back as Garrick, Anna Neagle was Peg and Jack Hawkins played Michael, her first admirer. The Regal showed Shirley Temple with the brilliant coloured dancer, Bill Robinson in *The Little Colonel*. *China Seas*, with the big box office team, Clark Gable and Jean Harlow, was at the Empire Theatre. Jean Harlow, the sex symbol of the period, did a good deal of symbolising and Clark Gable, on board a rusty tub battling through an oriental hurricane, was immaculate in white suit impeccably tailored (in Hong Kong, no doubt) unperturbed by wind and rain and the hundreds of Chinese milling uncomfortably around his ship.

Looking remarkably like Lawrence of Arabia, Walter Hudd was cast in the title role in the London Film production of *Lawrence of Arabia*. Tolstoy's *Anna Karenina* came to the screen in the person of Greta Garbo, Basil Rathbone playing her husband and Fredric March the male lead. In its first week in New York, 126,000 people paid money to see the movie. Fredric March turned up again in the Samuel Goldwyn production, *The Dark Angel*, with blossoming Merle Oberon. Paul Muni, star of *I am a Fugitive from a Chain Gang*, stopped running to appear as a Polish miner in *Black Fury*, a tense movie about life in the Pennsylvania coalfields. Edward G. Robinson was the proprietor of a crooked gambling den in Sam Goldwyn's *Barbary Coast*, and Shirley Temple's *Curly Top* followed singing star Grace Moore's *On the Wings of Song* at the Tivoli. Katharine Hepburn and French heart-throb Charles Boyer in *Break of Hearts* was blurbed as brilliant casting.

At the end of 1935 it was reported that superstar Constance Bennett,

Above, Jean Harlow. *Right*, George Arliss in *East Meets West*. *Far right*, Claudette Colbert and Clive Brook in *The Man From Yesterday*.

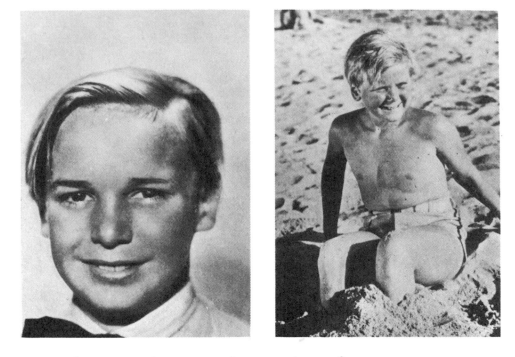

reputed to earn £6,000 a week portraying unfortunate women, was to
make films in Britain and though it was doubtful that such a sum could
be paid for her services in Britain, she was welcome as a refreshing
change from native stage stars who were unable to adapt themselves to
playing film roles and the semi-amateurs and dilettantes who got film
jobs on the strength of their social connections.

Midnight on 4 December 1935 saw the European premiere of *Broadway Melody of 1936* by Metro-Goldwyn-Mayer. The thin story line was
of a New York impresario who packed off his childhood sweetheart to
her hometown to spare her the pitfalls of Broadway, only to have her
return posing as a French star complete with phoney accent. But the
shrewd impresario, for the sake of the movie, failed to recognise his
childhood sweetheart and a star was born. The film featured spectacular production numbers with hundreds of dancers careering around
in ever diminishing circles to finally disappear into the auditorium,
good songs and Eleanor Powell, world's greatest tapdancer, even if she
could fool nobody except the impresario into believing she was French.
At the Carlton, *Top Hat* with song and dance team Fred Astaire and
Ginger Rogers was breaking all records.

Things to Come was made by London Film Productions from H. G.
Wells's novel and turned out to be an overrated, unconvincing sally
into the realms of the future, starting with a devastating war that went
on and on round a static Piccadilly-like set and wearily wound up with
a message of hope that impressed nobody. Another H. G. Wells film
was *The Man Who Could Work Miracles*, starring Gilbert Roland as a
draper's assistant endowed by three capricious supernatural beings
with power to work miracles. In *East Meets West*, a cunning oriental
potentate, the Sultan of Renang, alias George Arliss, was involved with

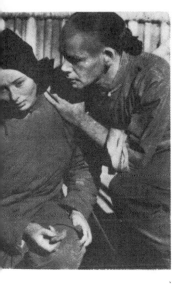

From left to right, Luise Rainer and Paul Muni in *The Good Earth*, 1937; young Peter Lawford, hailed as a new Jackie Coogan in 1931; Anna Neagle as the young queen in *Victoria the Great*, 1937.

the British government in negotiating over a potential naval base in his territory. Shades of Singapore. At the beginning of 1937, the film of Pearl Buck's *The Good Earth*, about peasant life in China, had its premiere at the Palace Theatre, London. Paul Muni as Wang and Luise Rainer as O-Lan, his wife, both made up with slit eyes in the standard depiction of Chinese, moved drearily through acres of hilly Californian countryside made to look like Chinese countryside under the expert supervision of a Californian Chinese farmer and, so publicity had it, amid ten thousand genuine Chinese employed as extras. This Metro-Goldwyn-Mayer motion picture was the last that Irving Thalberg ever produced. For their trouble in groping through the film squinting sorrowfully through slit eyes, Paul Muni and Luise Rainer were proclaimed by the Academy of Motion Picture Awards the greatest film actor and actress of 1936.

Under the Red Robe, film version of Stanley Weyman's romance, made at Denham, starred Conrad Veidt as a Gil de Berault and Annabella as the Lady Marguerite. Raymond Massey played a devious Cardinal Richelieu. In *His Affair* Victor McLaglen and Brian Donlevy were a pair of bank robbers in the nineties tracked down by a young naval officer played by Robert Taylor. Barbara Stanwyck was the female star. The film was about intrigue in the White House, with President McKinley giving the naval officer the task of sorting out the bank-robbers believed to be in league with a Washington big-wig.

The Lord Chamberlain revised the ban on plays and films dealing with Queen Victoria and right away Herbert Wilcox produced the film *Victoria the Great* starring Anna Neagle. All her robes for the film were correct down to the last detail and the greatest care was taken to 'ensure the accuracy of historical events'. In *One in a Million* world

39

champion ice skater, Sonja Henie made her Hollywood screen debut and her performance on ice was described as poetry in motion. Merle Oberon and Laurence Olivier starred in *The Divorce of Lady X*, and Ginger Rogers and Katharine Hepburn were teamed in *Stage Door*, a film about the ups and downs of some twenty show girls living in a boarding house for show people. Some fun.

The Plainsman, Cecil B. De Mille's super western starring Gary Cooper was about the days of Wild Bill Hickok, Indian raids and the relentless march of rapacious pioneers. In February 1938, Fredric March played the swashbuckling pirate, Jean Lafitte in *The Buccaneer*.

In *Blockade* with Henry Fonda and Madeleine Carroll the setting was the Spanish Civil War, still raging at the time. It was an unlikely, unrealistic story about espionage and counter-espionage. Margaret Lockwood and John Loder starred with Scottish comedian Will Fyffe and a sheepdog in *Owd Bob*, and Gracie Fields in *We're Going to be Rich*, a Twentieth Century Fox picture, played the well worn rollicking role of a big hearted variety artiste supporting her good-natured but ne'er-do-well husband all the way from Melbourne to Johannesburg in the good old days.

The Pulitzer Prize winning play by George S. Kaufman and Moss Hart, *You Can't Take it With You*, was brought to the screen by Frank Capra. The crazy Vanderhof menage included Lionel Barrymore as the old grandfather. James Stewart was Tony Kirby, Jean Arthur played Alice Sycamore and Edward Arnold was Anthony P. Kirby, the podgy-faced capitalist who, reluctantly brought to the conclusion that he could not take it with him, decided to make the best of it and not go. *Free to Live* was the story of Linden Seton, Katharine Hepburn, who tried to hide her love for her sister's fiancé, John Case, played by Cary Grant, a businessman with the not uncommon ambition to retire rich and early.

Comedy teams such as the Marx Brothers, the Ritz Brothers, and the Stooges, were popular. The Marx Brothers' movies such as *Animal Crackers*, *Duck Soup* and *A Night at the Opera* have, for some reason, come to be regarded as movie classics. Laurel and Hardy bumbling along in their own series of movies were also to receive wider acclaim in recent years.

Starting with Edward G. Robinson in the title role of *Little Caesar* in 1930, gangster movies were good box office throughout the hungry thirties. People seemed to derive some vicarious pleasure from the ruthless way gangsters could trample over the mores of snobbish society, ride rough shod over authority and the law, and assert power over the establishment. Often the supporting gangster roles were played by the same teams of movie gangsters, sympathetic characters always good for a laugh when not wasting someone or other, termed 'bumping off' in those far off days. Those jovial hoodlums included open faced Frank McHugh, puckish Edward Brophy, laconic Alan

A scene from *You Can't Take It With You.*

Shirley Temple.

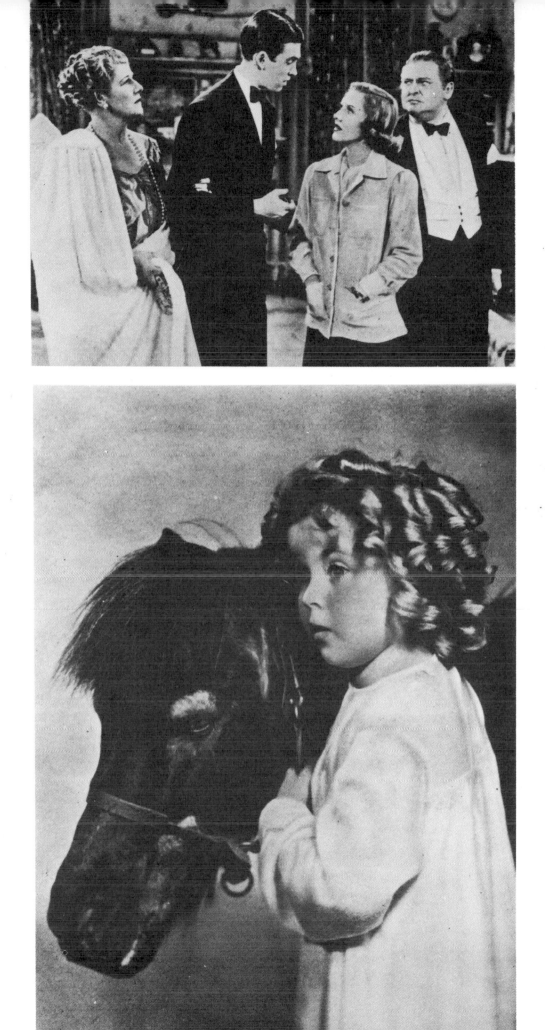

Jenkins, bald headed Vince Barnett and gravel voiced Lionel Stander. They were always on tap ready to supply humour to offset the basic baseness of sordid gangsterdom.

Spencer Tracy, Cary Grant, Bing Crosby, Dick Powell and Bette Davis were shining brightly as the lights were going out all over Europe. *Gone with the Wind* with Clark Gable, Vivien Leigh, Leslie Howard and Hattie McDaniel, was all set for a record breaking run and Judy Garland in *The Wizard of Oz* had the young men singing 'We're Off to See the Wizard, the Wonderful Wizard of Oz' as they marched to war.

The incomparable Josephine Baker, star of films, cabaret and stage, and Anna May Wong, Chinese star of the thirties.

42

Where are the boys of the old brigades?

The hero's red rag is laid across his eyes,
Lies by the Madrid rock and baptises sand,
Grander than God with the blood of his best and
Estremadura is blazing in his fallen hand.

ELEGY ON SPAIN George Barker.

WHEN I WAS STAYING ON A FARM NEAR HAILSHAM IN Sussex with my brother and two friends the Spanish Civil War started. We had just returned from a hike, dusty and footsore, when we heard about it on the radio and then sat down to a high tea with plenty of tomatoes, fresh baked bread and home-made jam, and appetites to go with it.

Sabre rattling, revolts, riots and even war were only too familiar. The Italians had already overrun Abyssinia, the Japanese were steadily wiping up China, Hitler was knocking holes in the drum and Black-shirts were running loose in London streets. Some politicians were whistling in the dark and optimistic, at least in public, about the prospects for peace, but I do not think that, in general, the youth of the period had any such illusions.

Insurrection in Spain in the thirties was nothing new, but before long this latest so-called insurrection blossomed into a full scale war in the horrific pattern of 1914–18. Men from all walks of life, all over the world flocked to Spain to fight, mostly on the side of the Republican government. Mussolini, the Bullfrog of the Pontine Marshes, puffed up with poisonous hot air, sent his Italian gun-fodder to join Franco's Moors in bolstering the rebellious forces, and Hitler supplied an air force and technicians to experiment and practise warfare on the body of Spain. Millions of ordinary Spaniards were soon embroiled in the bloodbath.

Newspapers had a busy time supplying maps of battle areas in Spain with arrows pointing in every direction, articles and leaders blowing

43

hot and cold, and harrowing accounts from Johnnies-on-the-spot. After a while many British newspapers began to side with the Spanish Government, falling out of step with their own.

As the war dragged on and grew more bitter, more and more volunteers from Europe, America and the British Isles went to join the international brigades of the Spanish Government. Soon we began hearing about casualties to the British battalion. Several boys I had known at school went off to fight in Spain. One was killed early in the defence of Madrid and another at bloody Jarama where the Madrilenos now go for a quiet weekend trout fishing. A professional boxer who, under the name of Phil Richards, I had often seen fight at the Premierland in London, and whose brother I knew very well, was killed at Jarama fighting for Republican Spain. We learned of other casualties from friends and relatives.

We all knew the song of the International Brigade, sung to the tune of 'Red River Valley', with words attributed to Alex McDade, a Glaswegian Brigader. Boys at school used to sing it:

> *There's a place in Spain called Jarama*
> *That's a place we all know so well,*
> *For 'tis there that we wasted our manhood*
> *And most of our old age as well.*

In working class areas vans went round the streets collecting clothing and canned foods to send to civilians in Republican Spain. Donations of money were collected and schemes were launched to raise funds to provide ambulances and medical supplies for the Spanish Government forces and especially for the British battalion, called the Saklatvala after Brixton's Indian Communist M.P., and later the Major Attlee battalion, after the man who was to become British Prime Minister less than a decade later.

In the end, the Britons who had fought bitter engagements in the resolute defence of Madrid, at Jarama and the Ebro, came home, happy to be home, unhappy at the outcome of the war in Spain which was rapidly drawing to its doleful conclusion. I saw them arrive in London, some minus an arm or a leg, some in wheelchairs – relics of a lost cause. I met a number of them on various occasions and listened to the stories they had to tell. Many years later, after World War Two, while staying in New York, I was taken to a roadhouse in Parisippany, New Jersey, by an American friend for a Thanksgiving dinner. He introduced me to a mild-mannered man a few years older than me, who had fought in the American Abraham Lincoln battalion of the International Brigade and later went over to Normandy on D-Day. He told me a good deal about the war in Spain, mostly about conditions behind the lines and about Britons he had met. I was struck by his particularly dispassionate account and the way he avoided questions.

Later my friend told me that the ex-soldier had experienced a very

Disorder in Seville in August 1932.

difficult time in the U.S. after his return from Spain and had lost several jobs because of his Spanish connections. Yet the man had never been a Communist. It was partly adventure that took him to Spain and he returned home disillusioned. Drafted during World War Two, he had served in France and Germany and returned home even more disillusioned. He had eventually found his niche, however. When, in 1953, Eisenhower, in a sweat over the cold war, decided to befriend France, the ex-Brigader had said 'To hell with it all', and following in Eisenhower's wake had become a public relations man for a big Spanish business organisation.

I have heard many first-hand accounts of the Civil War from Spaniards in Bilbao, Barcelona and Madrid. On several occasions I have visited the castillo which stands on the top of the Montana De Montjuich overlooking Barcelona. It was there that Franco packed political prisoners when his forces finally occupied the city on 26 January 1939. I have been to the Colon Hotel where Rebel troops barricaded themselves during the few days of fierce street fighting before the Rebels in Barcelona were overcome at the start of the War.

It was from a Basque in Bilbao that I first heard the strange story that the death of Franco's youngest brother, Ramon, killed when his plane crashed into the sea on 18 October 1938 had, in fact, been no accident. Ramon, who had become a hero in Spain when he had flown the South Atlantic in 1935, had developed left-wing associations and involvements. He had always been considered an embarrassment by his brother who tried to maintain a scrupulously immaculate image. At the time of his death, the flamboyant Ramon was in command of a Nationalist seaplane base in Majorca where he resented Italian inter-

Prelude to civil war – martial law in Seville in 1931.

46

At the barricades – in Madrid *above* where dead horses provided cover for rebel troops, and in Barcelona *right*.

ference and it was finally deemed expedient that Ramon should cease to be an embarrassment. Certainly, at Ramon's funeral, Franco showed no emotion whatsoever; not even satisfaction.

By the time Bilbao fell to Franco on 19 June 1938, fifteen thousand Basques had been killed in battle alone. I was told that Franco immediately ordered a mass parade of the Falange and Requetes in the occupied Basque capital, in which marched children with toy rifles, young girls conscripted for 'social' work, and fishermen, factory and office workers who were forced to take part. It was not long before thousands of political prisoners were being clapped in jail and workers were being murdered wholesale by vengeful Fascists.

I was told about the bombing of Guernica, a small town just north of Bilbao, by the Condor Legion of Franco's German allies. The Germans had demonstrated saturation bombing – one of the deadly experiments for which they have been notorious – with bombers flying in relays raining incendiaries and high explosives on the defenceless town of some seven thousand inhabitants, for three terrifying hours. The small market town was razed to the ground and a third of the inhabitants were killed or wounded. It was said that even the Insurgents were horrified by the world's reaction to news of the raid and Franco, pretending that he had had no knowledge that such a raid had been planned, managed to squeeze out one or two crocodile tears. To mollify those of his men who thought the raid had been a bad public relations exercise for Spain, he connived with the Germans to demonstrate his concern by having the commander of the Condor Legion recalled to Germany. Picasso painted his huge canvas 'Guernica', to commemorate the raid and I went to see it at the Whitechapel Art Gallery. An old man from Santander told me that until the fall of Bilbao, despite the so-called policy of non-intervention by the big powers, petrol and motor vehicles – mostly Fords and Studebaker

47

trucks – used to arrive for Franco from the U.S. through Lisbon.

Madrid is a beautiful city, very hot in summer, very cold in winter. On the northern outskirts, the ruins of University City have been replaced by impressive buildings and gardens and it is difficult to realise that bitter fighting took place there and in the vicinity practically throughout the whole of the Civil War. Spanish Tourist Office brochures have never mentioned the fighting in and around Madrid and that at one time Moroccans were reported to have penetrated to the Plaza Espana; that Nationalist tanks ventured down the Calle de la Princesa from University City and that across the Manzanares were Nationalist trenches in the beautiful Caso De Campo, Madrid's largest park.

On 7 November 1936 an army composed mainly of Moroccans and Spanish Foreign Legionaries attacked Madrid. The inhabitants awoke that frightening morning to the deafening crescendo of bombardment by artillery that heralded the beginning of the ordeal and agony the city was to suffer for almost the next three years. That baptism of gunfire rallied the citizens of Madrid. They worked unceasingly all day building barricades, organising defences while the Fascists kept pressing closer. On the morning of 8 November 1936 between two and three thousand men, the first battalions of the international brigades, marched along the Gran Via toward University City to stop the enemy dead in their tracks. The Madrilenos took fresh heart.

I knew a Romanian who served with the international brigades, and fought at Madrid, Jarama, Teruel and on the Ebro. He was among those who were subsequently forced across the border into France and wound up in a French camp which he vowed was worse than any he had ever been in, and he had been in a few. To get out of it, he joined the French Foreign Legion in time to fight the Germans in Northern France in 1940. He was with the few Frenchmen who were shipped to England from Dunkirk. He joined the Free French forces and was back in France on D-Day in 1944.

This Romanian had many tales to tell, amusing and otherwise. He swore that at University City the enemy was so close that at nightfall, many of them used to infiltrate the Republican lines to visit brothels in Madrid and he hoped that they had all caught the pox and died. He said that as for the Italians, the only ones that had fought well were those in the Garibaldi battalion in XII International Brigade. Mussolini's unwilling minions with Franco used spaghetti for bootlaces and were more proficient with mandolines than with machine guns. He referred to their air force as the 'bambino bombers'.

I visited La Vallee de los Caidos (The Valley of the Fallen) about thirty miles north of Madrid, where a cross 150 metres high stands over a vast subterranean church and overlooks the broad expanses of a cemetery and the wild hollows around it. The whole monstrous edifice, built at Cuelgamuros between the Escorial and Guadarrama by the

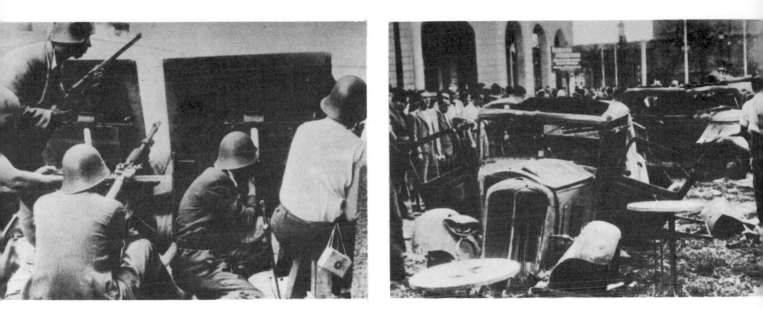

Barcelona, July 1936.
Pictured *right* is the Plaza
Cataluna.

sweated labour of Franco's political prisoners, is hypocritically dedicated to the memory of those who 'died for Spain'. The final obscenity was the pollution of the valley by the burying there of the body of Franco, the man most responsible for putting them in their graves.

Slick design of the ornate church is vaguely reminiscent of the impressive Ossuary at Douamont, near Verdun in France, but it is really no more than a tourist trap. Together with a number of other people, my wife and I went into a café outside the cavern for something to drink. We came out to sit at one of the tables only to be seen off in no uncertain manner by a snarling waiter who insisted that nobody who had not been served by him and who had not suitably tipped him could use a table. When I pointed out that none of us had realised this and in any case, he had been dozing in a corner when we had come out of the cavern, he disappeared round the back of the café and returned triumphantly with a policeman, guard or whatever, to back him up which he did splendidly, spitting and spluttering like a sparkler. We would not have been at all surprised had he reached for his holster and drawn his pistol. So much for the overawing spectacle of the Vallee de los Caidos.

There are more ominous reminders of the Spanish Civil War than the Valley of the Fallen, all over Spain, but perhaps they will disappear one day with the release of political prisoners from Spanish jails and the return to Spain of political freedom. The Spaniards in uniform I have encountered in Spain are, without a doubt, a special breed. Most of them seem to have been petty tyrants who had been given their jobs because of their political affiliations, nepotism or judicious back-handers. For example the park-keeper in the Cactus gardens on the side of Montjuich who, when his eagle eye spotted a tourist inadvertently putting a toe over the grass verge, nearly blew the pea right out of his whistle, then shouted, raged and waved his fist menacingly. I saw

49

another 'parkie' in Tarragona give a dressing-down to a harmless labourer who had been taking a lunchtime nap on a bench on a clifftop overlooking the sea. And there was the homunculus dressed in a cut-down police uniform who surely could not have been a policeman but was. I saw him lording it in Sitges where he seemed to be on every corner snarling up at someone or other. And the policeman at Barajas Airport who testily waved me away when I asked him the way to the john. And the Civil Guard in Bilbao who stopped abruptly in his tracks and glared at me, belligerently fingering the flap of his pistol holster when I happened to glance curiously at his leather hat.

Perhaps I was the one who was hypercritical, but it did not look that way to me from my side of the counter.

General Cabanellas, head of the Spanish rebel provisional government in 1936.

A small group of British volunteers went into action on the side of the government practically as soon as the war started and fought well alongside volunteers from France and Germany in the early defence of Madrid. Among those men were John Summerfield and Bernard Knox; the sensitive poet John Cornford and Winston Churchill's adventurous nephew Esmond Romilly. When, in November and December 1936, more British volunteers arrived at the Republican training centre at Madrigueras, some of them were selected to form the first all-British company, with a stiffening of British veterans of Madrid such as George Nathan and Cornford. Before the year was out, the company, designated Number One Company in the twelfth French battalion of the XIVth International Brigade, was in action at Lopera on the Andujar front.

Ill-equipped with old French and Austrian weapons, the British managed to advance to the outskirts of Lopera, but were thrown back. On 29 December the whole battalion went into the attack against the Escorial road. Bombed, shelled and machine gunned and suffering severe casualties in six hours of bloody combat, the British company was compelled to retire. Attack followed counter attack and after nearly a month of fighting, sixty-seven survivors of the one hundred and forty-five men who had originally marched out of Madrigueras returned from the front to rest – battered, bedraggled, haggard and weary – but not twenty-one year-old Cornford who had written only a few weeks earlier:

> And if bad luck should lay my strength
> In the shallow grave,
> Remember all the good you can;
> Don't forget my love.

He was already resting in his shallow grave.
However, by now there were six hundred Britons in the training

Women flock to join the government militia in Barcelona in 1936.

camp getting ready for the front. These men from all walks of life included Fred Copeman who, as an able seaman, had been the leader of the naval mutiny at Invergordon, for which he had been given a long jail sentence, ex-sailor Sam Wilde and Jock Cunningham, a former sergeant in the Argyll and Sutherland Highlanders.

In January 1937 the newly formed British battalion, composed of four rifle companies and specialist units, was ready for the front, but the day before it was due to leave, the Brigade Commander, André Marty, had trouble with the Irish section and on the morning of the day that the British battalion was due to march off, it was decided that

51

Spanish Foreign Legionaries and Moorish troops in southern Spain in September 1936.

its commander should be replaced because, at a meeting of brigade commanders, a conclusion had been reached that it would not be politic, after all, to let the battalion go into its first action commanded by a non-Communist. Wilfred Macartney, the Battalion Commander, refused to relinquish his command and was thereupon summoned to appear at headquarters. On the way by car he was accidentally shot with his own pistol and wounded.

Macartney, ex-officer in the British army in World War One, courier, adventurer, playboy, alleged Communist and spy for Russia, had served a long sentence in a British jail and was out on parole when he went to Spain. A brief account of his career appears in the previous book in this series.

Tom Wintringham took over command of the British battalion and it finally marched off for the Jarama front on a cold January night to take up positions alongside French, Italian, Czech, Austrian and Balkan volunteers. On the night of 11 February the Fascists launched ten thousand men supported by heavy artillery fire at Jarama. The British were ordered to counter-attack, but immediately came under furious fire and before long, found themselves without support on either flank.

However, on 14 February the British smashed an attack by Moors but on the right, the Nationalists were forcing back the Edgar André, Dimitrov and Thaelman battalions, causing them heavy casualties, including the commanders of both the Edgar André and Thaelman battalions. The French counter-attacked and also incurred terrible

52

Moorish troops fly from Spanish Morocco to fight for the rebels.

losses. The entire XIth International Brigade was in danger of disintegrating, but officers and brigade commissars rallied the men and the line held.

Wintringham's part in the battle was not going according to plan and there was a good deal of confusion. Number Four Company had turned to flee, allowing the Fascists to penetrate to the rear of Number One Company. Many of the British were wounded, killed or taken prisoner. Wintringham was wounded in one leg and sent to the rear.

Copeman organised a group of machine guns just in time to engage masses of red-turbanned Moors pouring down from the hills to attack the Republican lines. The British gunners mowed them down in waves and soon the survivors were trying to crawl to cover under a deadly steel lash that whipped around them mercilessly. In the lull that followed, Copeman went behind the lines to round up stragglers and deserters and managed to lead a group of one hundred men back to the front.

In the main, the spirited British defence discouraged the Fascists and they hesitated while Republican reinforcements were moving up, but British casualties were mounting. Jock Cunningham had taken over command from Wintringham and was conferring with Copeman about resiting the Maxim guns when a group of Moors, dressed in uniforms of the International Brigade and singing the 'Internationale', succeeded in bluffing the Maxim crews who, before they could recover from their surprise, found themselves taken prisoner. The battalion was down from six hundred to one hundred and eighty men but Jock Cunning-

53

ham rushed his exhausted men to fill the gap in the line made by the Moors where Copeman, with a mere handful of men and two French field guns, was trying to maintain some sort of defence.

The British swept forward and almost succeeded in reaching part of their former positions but the Fascists pressed hard all around them. Soon, only just over one hundred British remained standing, battling with grenades and small arms against overwhelming odds. Just when it seemed that their situation was hopeless, Lister's Spanish brigade appeared on the Moorish left flank and soon Franco's Moors were running for their lives. To the north the Nationalist attack ran out of steam and the enemy was driven back to the Jarama River by the XIth International Brigade, composed mostly of Germans and the Balkan soldiers of the Dimitrov battalion.

But there was no respite. The fighting continued with attack and counter-attack until a stalemate was reached when each side had lost about half of its strength. The surviving British in their sector dug in with the Lister brigade, the Jarama separating them from the Fascists. The men gradually deepened and extended their weapon pits into a trench system with sandbags, revetments and machine gun emplacements, then settled down to the grim uncomfortable monotony of life in the trenches. There was desultory shelling at times, but the front was mainly quiet and as the months passed and the weather grew warmer, men were able to sunbathe, play table tennis and even football in the deep hollows to the rear of the trenches.

There were British in other units of the International Brigades who saw service on various other fronts and sectors during this period, but in July they all returned to Albacete where the XVth International Brigade was being formed for a big offensive at Brunete.

Below, rebels near Irun in September 1936. *Below right*, a rebel mule battery advancing towards San Marital. *Opposite*, surrender of loyalists at Somosiena on the Guadarrama front.

54

The defence of Madrid, 1937. *Right*, trenches on the outskirts. *Opposite*, the International Brigade in the suburbs. *Below*, trenches in University City.

In the north, the Basques were being hard pressed and Bilbao was in danger. The government decided to launch two offensives to relieve the pressure on the Basque city. Implementing their plans was not easy. The government was beset by troubles due to political disunity, incompetence and some internal strife between irresponsible and disruptive factions. However, the operations as envisaged by Rojo, Government Chief of Staff, involved a pincer movement starting from the north and east toward Mostales and deploying 80,000 men, seven hundred pieces of artillery and some two hundred aircraft. The drive from the north through Brunete involved the use of the XVth International Brigade which was divided into two regiments. One, led by the immaculate ex-Guards officer George Nathan, included the Lincoln battalion commanded by Merriman, the George Washington battalion commanded by a negro, Oliver Law, and the British battalion commanded by Fred Copeman.

56

Lister's 11th Division led the attack on 6 July, swiftly penetrating the enemy lines advancing to Brunete and beyond, but soon the breach was clogged with milling troops and vehicles as in a confusion of conflicting orders the brigades were poured through to meet Nationalist reinforcements head on. Republican tanks were squandered assaulting useless objectives and as the Fascists, reacting rapidly, brought up battalions of fresh troops, supported by field artillery, the Republican advance slowed and then ground to a halt, resolving into a vicious struggle under a burning sun. Corpses roasted and burst on the blood soaked Castilian plain. Dying men cried out their final agonies, wounded cried out in vain for water.

The tired, dirty and thirsty men of the British battalion of the XVth International Brigade, after a gruelling night march, were thrown into the attack, with Villanueva de la Canada as the first objective. The early morning sun was hot when Fred Copeman, at the head of his men, advanced across open country and as the sun crept up the sky and grew hotter, the British began to suffer terribly from thirst. Water bottles, sent to the rear to be filled before the advance, had not been returned but the troops pressed on and eventually Villanueva, pounded by Republican artillery and wraithed in dust, loomed ahead.

The men crouched in ditches and dried-out gullies to gather strength before the final onslaught. Then, as they rose, wet with sweat and caked with dust, they came under intense fire from enemy snipers and machine gunners and their casualties began to mount rapidly. Copeman ordered his men to go to ground and wait for nightfall. At twilight, an attempt by some Italian troops to infiltrate the British positions, using women and children as cover, was thwarted. The British then continued their advance which carried them into the blazing streets of Villanueva de la Canada where they linked up with troops of another brigade.

The next day the XVth International Brigade resumed its forward movement as the enemy crossed the Guadarrama River to take up fresh positions, but conditions were worsening for the attackers. As the British advanced in an attempt to take the vital Mosquito Ridge, they were met by a shattering artillery bombardment. Frantically, the men scattered, scrabbling for cover as shells bursting all around them flung jagged fragments of white hot metal whining over their heads. Bombers of the Condor Legion joined in the bombardment and the troops, pinned to the shuddering earth, tormented by hunger and thirst, cringed in pulsating terror. Blood soaked wounded had to suffer where they lay until nightfall when stretcher bearers dared to creep forward in an effort to carry them to comparative safety.

As the skull-splitting roar of the barrage was dying down, the British started to move forward again over the ridges and were within sight of their objective when, once more, a terrific air and artillery bombardment stopped them in their tracks and for hours the tortured

Opposite, the fall of Bilbao to Franco in June 1937.

58

Rebel troops, 1938.

Spanish government
commander, General Rojo.

men were forced to hug the quivering earth as great gouts of dirt and flames plumed skyward.

But as the barrage ceased, the British moved doggedly on although still under tremendous enemy pressure until, after relieving the Washington battalion, they found themselves dangerously exposed in advance of all other units. It was now obvious to them that without support they had no chance of taking Mosquito Ridge and, as the whole Republican advance shuddered to a halt and Fascist counter-

60

attacks were beaten off with difficulty, food and ammunition began to run low. After forty-eight hours, in the face of strong enemy resistance, heavy casualties, hunger and thirst, the British were forced to withdraw. In eight days of fighting, their strength had been reduced from 630 to 185 men. The outcome of the battle was that for a gain of a few battered villages, the Republicans lost 24,000 dead.

The second offensive, designed to relieve the pressure on the Basques, was launched by the government along the Aragon front on 24 August, with Zaragoza as the objective. The XVth International Brigade was only a twentieth of the forces engaged in the battle (which was almost a repeat of the Battle of Brunete) but the chance to exploit brilliant breakthroughs was bedevilled by petty squabbles and jealous intrigues within the Republican military and political wings.

The British battalion was held in reserve while the Lister Brigade cut Nationalist communications at the rear of Quinto and the American, loyal Spanish and Dimitrov battalions moved in to occupy the town. The British were given the task of launching the final assault on the strategic Purburell Hill.

At the start of the British attack, their advancing infantry immediately came under intense fire from the Fascist lines. Peter Daly, the Irish commander, was hit and died later in hospital. Casualties were severe and the attack was called off until the next day. At dawn, the advance started again and in the face of enfilading machine gun fire from well-sited emplacements, and tangles of barbed wire which Republican artillery had failed to destroy, the assault swept forward and dozens of Fascist prisoners were taken.

The attack on Belchite in the South was developing and the Spanish XXXII Brigade was incurring casualties at an alarming rate. The XVth International Brigade was called upon to try to recapture the initiative and it fell to the Lincoln battalion to bear the brunt of the fighting. After a while, the XVth International Brigade was withdrawn from the front to rest, but on 12 October it was ordered up to the Fuentes del Ebro front to take part in an attempt to smash past the Fascist fortifications toward Zaragoza. The attack opened on 13 October and was across open ground, the men climbing slowly toward the enemy trenches. But the expected artillery and air support failed to materialise. Nevertheless, the attack proceeded and for the first time an assault was attempted by tanks carrying infantry and troops in trucks. The troops were British, Canadian and American.

The tanks broke through the enemy lines all right, but the Nationalists closed round the gap and met the troop-laden trucks with such an appalling concentration of fire that they wilted in their tracks, disgorging the defenceless troops who rushed madly for cover. The Spaniards riding on the tanks were then picked off and the tanks, miles behind enemy lines and out of petrol, were blasted into submission or destroyed. The new technique of tank and motorborne infantry to spearhead an attack was sound enough, as the Germans were later to demonstrate in their blitzkriegs. The Spanish operation failed mainly because of lack of adequate radio communications, language difficulties in transmitting orders, insufficient co-ordination and the inability to provide swift flanking forces.

After a good deal of confused fighting in which the British covered the flank of the Lincoln battalion, the Republican advance came to a standstill and it was seen that there was no hope of it continuing. As night fell, the survivors of the abortive attack made their way back and they hastily dug in less than a mile in front of their old start line. On 3 October they were ordered to the rear and a Spanish brigade took over.

While Franco was nearing final preparations for his Guadalajara-Alcala offensive, the Republicans struck, beating him to the punch. On 15 December, in falling snow, an attack was launched against the enemy salient around the city of Teruel, north and east of the point where Franco had concentrated his forces. Lister's 11th Division led the assault without artillery and air support, hoping to surprise the enemy, and Heredia's XVIIIth Brigade struck out as the other claw to a pincer movement. By the evening, Teruel was the scene of violent street fighting. Instead of rushing through the town in pursuit of the enemy and cutting it off to be mopped up by support troops later, the government forces allowed themselves to become bogged down in the narrow streets. Franco had to make a quick decision, whether to withdraw to positions far in the rear or to retake Teruel and push the Republicans right back to the Alfambra River.

Franco's decision was to launch a counter-offensive and it opened on 29 December under cover of the German Condor Legion. The Republicans yielded ground and the international brigades, which had for a while been held back for various political reasons, were ordered up in reserve.

The weather was atrocious. A fierce blizzard covered the roads with over four feet of snow in places, with drifts piling up. The cold was intense, almost twenty degrees below zero. Guns and vehicles were frozen and immobilised and misery bore down upon the troops, many of whom succumbed to frostbite. The Nationalist counter-offensive was frozen to a halt on 8 January 1938 and Nationalist survivors who were trapped in Teruel were forced to surrender. Franco was again faced with the option of making a substantial withdrawal or a concentrated effort to 'press on regardless'. On 15 January Franco's forces lashed out and now it was the Republicans in Teruel who were in danger. Two days later, Franco's generals launched a second counter-offensive with the heights above Teruel as the objective. On the following day, after a relentless pounding of the Republican lines by Italian artillery, the Republicans wilted and the Fascists broke through. It was then that the international brigades, under General Walker, were ordered into

Above, Teruel captured by government forces in January 1938. *Top right*, Falangist headquarters, Teruel. *Right*, government troops in trenches outside Teruel.

battle.

The men of the Major Attlee battalion were strung across the upper slopes of snow-covered mountain ridges overlooking the valley and the main road into Teruel. The Canadian battalion commanded a similar position below the British, and Spanish Republicans occupied the more strategic hill positions. A pulverising bombardment forced the Spanish from the hills and Fascists moved in to occupy them, but ran into a withering storm of British machine gun fire. The Fascists attacked again and British riflemen came running down the slope in a desperate counter-attack but they failed to recapture the hills, though they did succeed in holding off the enemy.

The next day, after a preliminary bombardment, the Nationalists threw in another attack, this time against the Canadians who, however,

63

Fuentes de Ebro on the Aragon front, May 1938. *Far right,* Franco troops on the Ebro.

stood firm. The Fascists, in fury, hurled themselves against the British riflemen in the valley, who had counter-attacked on the previous day, and there was close fighting for a while. During a short lull, as they were trying to dig in, the British came under heavy artillery fire and had to shelter in their shallow weapon pits.

But the Nationalist General Yague with his African Army Corps reached the Alafamba River and, flinging a bridgehead across, threatened Republican road and rail communications with Valencia. Teruel's defences cracked and the Republicans, including the Republican commander El Campesino and his staff, had to fight their way out, leaving behind large supplies of arms and ammunition and ten thousand of their number dead in the ruined streets and buildings. There followed the usual recriminations among the dozens of factions whose constant wrangling racked the Republican body. All blamed everyone but themselves for the heavy government defeat and the loss of Teruel at a time when a closing of the ranks and rapid reorganisation might have mitigated against worse disasters yet to come.

On 9 March Franco struck yet again. After an intense aerial and artillery bombardment, Yague spearheaded the advance moving rapidly down the right bank of the Ebro. Further south, motorised Italians, as usual, ran into trouble but, despite themselves, somehow managed to pierce the Republican lines. General Rojo reorganised his forces to meet the threats and flung in all the international brigades but already swift enemy thrusts were slicing through the Republican lines of communication preventing closer co-operation between the complex units of the Republican forces.

The British, marching to take up positions in the Calaceite sector,

ran headlong into a company of Italian whippet tanks. In the fighting that followed British machine gunners gave a good account of themselves, destroying two tanks, but one hundred British were cut off and captured. By now, the Republican retreat had become almost a rout with Nationalists in the north pouring into Catalonia. Moroccans stormed into Lerida where, after desperate hand-to-hand fighting and obstinate resistance by Republican snipers, the government troops were forced to yield. Also, despite the usual task of having to pull the Italians' chestnuts out of the fire, this time at Tortosa where the Italians had got themselves into trouble, Franco's forces advanced thirty miles along a front of some sixty miles and succeeded in reaching the Mediterranean at Vinaroz, thus cutting the government forces in two. In six weeks Franco had achieved a notable victory. Not only had he split the government forces in the field, but he had split further the ever widening cracks in the whole structure of the Republican government itself.

By May, Franco's advance had been brought almost to a halt due to heavy Nationalist casualties and communications problems. Nevertheless, at the end of July another thrust to the south brought the Nationalists within striking distance of Valencia, seat of the Republican government. Its capture seemed certain. Preparing for this final assault on Valencia, Franco stopped his forces on the Ebro, confident that the river was sufficient barrier to any possible government attack from that direction.

But once more the Republicans proved their resilience and courage. On 25 July at 12.15 a.m. they launched a massive offensive across the Ebro. In the darkness of the night, thousands of Republican troops

Above, Moroccan troops in Bilbao. *Above right,* government tanks in Teruel.

swarmed across the river either in boats or by hastily constructed pontoon bridges. The Canadians were one of the first battalions of the XVth International Brigade to get across the river and were soon followed by the British and Americans. The British moved off in the direction of Corbera and when they made contact with the XIIIth Brigade and learned that Moors in the hills were denying their entry into the town, the British attacked and after an all night battle, routed the Moors. The XIIIth Brigade was able to occupy Corbera. Republican thrusts from three bridgeheads sent the Fascists reeling back, but the stifling heat of the day sapped the energy of friend and foe alike, slowing advance and retreat.

At the centre, Lister soon reached the outskirts of Gandesa, but by now, Franco was moving up massive reinforcements and despite a vigorous day and night assault, Lister was unable to capture the town. Furious fighting centred around a group of fortified hills and the XVth International Brigade was hurled into the attack against a key position, a hill called the Pimple. For five consecutive days British, Canadians, Americans, Slavs and Spaniards launched assault after assault against the stubbornly defended position and on the last day, the British were still maintaining their pressure – driving nearer and nearer to the top of the objective under murderous fire.

Number Two Company lost four acting commanders in five days of battle and the acting commander at the time of the last assault, Lieutenant Lewis Clive, was killed later. An Oxford rowing blue, he had won the double sculls in the Los Angeles Olympics in 1932. Also killed in the action was David Guest, son of Dr Haden Guest, M.P. for Islington, who had taken a first class honours in mathematics at

Cambridge and had originally gone to Spain to take up a teaching post.

By 2 August, the breakthrough had been contained, and enemy artillery and bombers severely punished the Republicans, forcing them to yield ground until, once more, they had little to show for their bloody effort. While the Ebro battle had been raging, news reached the XVth International Brigade that all the international brigades were to be withdrawn from Spain. By January 1939, most of the international brigades had left Spain and six months later Franco was standing on the body of Spain with his foot planted firmly on the throat.

Like the British, small groups of American volunteers served with the Spanish Republican forces months before the formation of an all-American battalion of the international brigades. When Americans from all over the U.S. began to arrive in Spain not long after the outbreak of the Spanish Civil War, they were sent to Villanueva de la Jara near Albacete for some rudimentary military training. Nationalist pressure was already increasing alarmingly and the government sorely needed fresh troops for the front. The man selected to train the Americans was Robert Hale Merriman, a graduate of Nevada University who had been studying in Europe when the Civil War started.

Despite many difficulties and personal animosities, after five weeks of training, the Americans were sent to Albacete where, after being briefed at the famous bull ring, they were issued with weapons and other equipment and packed off to the village of Chinchon above the Jarama valley. This force of five hundred Americans formed part of the XVth International Brigade.

At this time, the Republican forces were under extremely heavy pressure as German tanks headed up the Jarama toward the key Arganda bridge, while the Moors were moving in to encircle Madrid. Then the bridge was captured and the enemy smashed into the French André Marty battalion. The French, outnumbered and inadequately armed, fought for hours until they finally ran out of ammunition. Then, except for a handful of men who were taken prisoner, they were massacred by the Moors. But the Republicans fought back and the new XVth International Brigade, commanded by Colonel Gal, a Hungarian, went into action for the first time.

Major Merriman and his five hundred and twenty-seven men were moved up in a convoy of trucks to the outskirts of Morata where they came under air attack and received their baptism of fire. When the Americans finally arrived at Jarama a fierce battle was still in progress with the Republicans preparing to launch a counter-attack. The American Lincoln battalion took over positions from a Loyalist Spanish brigade near Morata on 23 February 1937 and the men were immediately ordered into the attack. They came under blistering fire from the Fascists and were pinned down. Number One Company did manage to push forward but as darkness fell over the battlefield, strewn

67

Americans on the Morata
front in August 1937.

American machine gunner
on the Morata front.

68

American machine gunner of the Lincoln battalion.

with dead and dying and the wounded crying piteously for help, it was clear that the American attack had failed.

On 27 February the battered Lincoln battalion was in reserve close to the British sector when it came under sniper fire which killed Alonzo Watson, the first American negro volunteer to die in Spain. A new attack was ordered to straighten the line. Straightening lines is a favourite dodge of leaders of all armies and millions of men must have died all over the world straightening lines to make neater maps for generals.

The men of the Spanish XXIVth Brigade were the first to move off. They clambered from their trenches and started stumbling forward but were stopped only a few yards from their trenches by a spiteful rain of bullets. The Lincolns were then ordered forward, although Merriman protested against the order, sending his men to almost certain death. Nevertheless, he led his five hundred across no man's land and was soon struck by a bullet in the shoulder. Enfilading fire from machine guns cut swathes in the ranks of the Americans and their casualties were frightening. Wounded men crawled, gasping, to their trenches. Still the murderous fire from the Fascists poured into the bewildered

69

The nationalists reach
Vinaroz on the
Mediterranean coast, June
1938.

Americans. Dead men jerked under the impact of machine gun bullets.
Casualties were mounting rapidly. It was beginning to drizzle as the
Americans rallied and fought on. By the evening, the rain was falling
steadily, soaking the shaken, miserable men crouching in shell holes or
shallow muddy pits waiting for darkness to give them a chance to snake
back to the comparative safety of their original positions.

On 14 March, supported by tanks, the Nationalists attacked the
Jarama defences. The line buckled but held. On 5 April a Republican
assault was ordered to straighten the line. The Lincolns, of whom only
one hundred and fifty-five men of the original five hundred remained,
the rest being replacements, at first supplied the covering fire. Then
they were ordered to move into the attack with the rest of the brigade.
They managed to reach their objective but once again their casualties
were grievous. In the long lull that followed, the Americans, like their
British comrades, sought to amuse themselves playing table tennis in
the hollows behind the trenches and sunbathing as the weather grew
warmer.

With the reforming of the XVth International Brigade under the
command of a Croat named Copic, the brigade was divided into two
regiments, one of which comprised the Abraham Lincoln, the George
Washington and British battalions. The whole brigade was then sent to
take part in the offensive toward Brunete. Merriman was once more in
command of the Lincolns, and Oliver Law commanded the Washingtons.

The Americans, alongside the British, took part in the attack on
Villanueva de la Canada and their casualties were crippling. Among
the hundreds of Americans killed was the coloured fighter, Oliver Law.

It was said that the outmoded arrowhead formation adopted by the Americans contributed to their heavy losses. Only about fifty per cent of the Lincolns and the Washingtons were still standing when the roll was called during a brief respite in the battle and the two groups of survivors were merged to form the famous Lincoln-Washington battalion.

The newly formed battalion was ostensibly in reserve when the Fascists started their counter-offensive, but the Americans soon found themselves locked in bloody combat as the Nationalists smashed through the Republican lines. For forty-eight hours, the Lincoln-Washingtons fought back, yielding ground grudgingly. The roads to their rear were clogged with retreating government vehicles, ambulances and troops. After weeks of continuous fighting and forced marches, the Americans managed to dig in. Almost immediately they were ordered to march another eight miles to Quijona where loyalist Spanish troops were almost surrounded. However, the Spaniards managed to fight their way out of the trap and in the nick of time, the order to the American troops was countermanded.

On 25 August, the reorganised American battalion, led by Hans Amlie, an engineer from Wisconsin, took part in a new offensive on the Aragon front. The Americans went into the attack with government tanks grinding down the Fascist defences. By the following morning, the Lincoln-Washingtons had fought their way into the streets of Quinto, 'mouseholing' from house to house and meeting the Fascists with rifles, knives, grenades and even sticks of dynamite. However, as enemy reinforcements began to encircle the town, the Americans withdrew.

71

The 'bambino bombers',
Italian Savoia-Marchetis in
Spain, 1938.

A few days later the Lincoln-Washingtons assaulted the heights overlooking Purburrel hill. At the foot of the hill they made contact with
the British who had been attacking Purburrel hill itself. Then the
Americans were once more pushed against Quinto and using nitro-
glycerine, they blasted the enemy strongpoints and succeeded in
capturing the town.

Next came the attack on Belchite where practically every ruined
building was a fortress. The Lincoln-Washingtons came to the rescue of
the Spanish XXXIInd Brigade, only to find themselves pinned down
by vicious Nationalist fire from the cathedral. Despite desperate night
attacks, the Americans were forced to yield ground. The Americans
subsequently attacked again and again until they succeeded in smash-

ing the Fascists back through the town. The fighting was fierce and bloody; devastation and the smell of death were everywhere. Avoiding the bullet swept streets, the Americans again 'mouscholed' their way through the houses and finally met Spanish loyalists advancing from the other side of town. The cathedral was surrounded and after a furious but futile defence, the Fascists surrendered. Robert Merriman, now the American Chief of Staff of the XVth International Brigade, was wounded six times in the assault.

The Brigade was withdrawn from the front for rest and reorganisation but on 12 October was ordered up to the Fuentes del Ebro for a new attack. The next day the attack began with an advance across open ground, but the promised air and artillery support failed to materialise and the Fascists were holding strong positions. The Lincoln-Washingtons advanced on the right flank of the Canadian battalion, the Mackenzie-Papineau, while the British covered the American flank toward the river, but it soon became painfully clear that the attack was going to fail. The fighting became confused and the Lincolns and Mac-Paps were forced to get their heads down and wait for darkness for a chance to get out of the death trap.

On 15 December Lister's 11th Division led the attack on Teruel and on 29 December, a Franco counter-attack threw the Republicans back. The weather was bitterly cold and deep snow covered the valleys when a second major Nationalist offensive, preceded by violent Italian artillery bombardment and German aerial support, burst against the Republican lines. On 18 January 1938 the line gave way and the international brigades under General Walter were ordered into action to stem the enemy tide.

73

A Cuban serving with the American battalion peers through a periscope.

Within a few days the Americans were in the thick of the fighting in and around the battered ruins of Teruel. The XVth International Brigade was relieved on 3 February, but on 9 February, the Nationalists launched a new counter-attack and the Brigade was called back into action for an assault on Fascist fortifications overlooking Segura. The Brigade had limited success but on 17 February, the final battle for Teruel began and more than fourteen thousand Republicans were trapped in the town and had to fight their way out.

On 9 March, Franco launched a new attack on the Aragon and the international brigades were moved up to the line. On the night the Lincolns were positioned on the hills, facing the line of the enemy advance, they heard that the Nationalists with their tanks had broken through the Republican lines in the Calceite sector. Before long, they realised that they themselves were surrounded and that their only chance was to smash their way out of the encirclement and join the defending forces in Gandesa. The Americans hurled themselves against the enemy, but only one company managed to break through. The others, held up by concentrated machine gun fire, waited until dark to try to infiltrate the Nationalist lines. However, in the darkness, groups of Americans became separated and one group, in a brush with the enemy, lost Major Merriman, one of the toughest American veterans of the XVth International Brigade.

After the rout, all that remained of the American battalion was fewer than forty men. Over four hundred were dead or missing. Once again the battalion had to be reformed but now, with so few American replacements, the new battalion had four Spaniards for every American. One new recruit to the new Lincoln-Washington battalion was Jim Lardner, son of Ring Lardner, the famous American writer.

In July the battalions took part in the desperate Republican offensive across the Ebro. The Americans were involved in bloody fighting in an area where hundreds of corpses rotted in stifling heat and unattended wounded blistered and died; this polluted area came to be known as Death Valley.

The battle had reached a climax when news arrived at the front that the international brigades were to be disbanded and the men repatriated. The last American action was on 22 September and among the heavy casualties was Jim Lardner, killed in action.

For the international brigades the war was over; for the rest of the Republican forces it was 'all over bar shouting'; for the big powers who had hoped to avoid war by hypocritical policies of non-intervention and appeasement, it was just about to begin.

Follow the band

Al Bowlly.

Sam Browne.

MY PARENTS TOOK THEMSELVES OFF TO LITTLEHAMPTON with my two youngest brothers on 27 August 1939. War was imminent and massive air raids were expected. My parents thought it would take some weeks to settle the children into a new place to stay. Meanwhile, I and my other two brothers, Dick and Stan, stayed at home. Three friends whose parents too had 'evacuated', came to stay with us.

There we were, six boys anticipating joining the Forces, with a house to ourselves and a 'who cares now?' attitude. When war broke out a week later, we were well organised. During the day we went to work; in the evening we cooked convenient meals, 'mucked in' with the chores and amused ourselves often until the early hours of the morning. With places of entertainment closed and a claustrophobic blackout of the streets, we had to provide our own pastimes. We played cards, invited in friends and took turns to keep the gramophone fully wound.

One of the friends staying with us, Harold Davison, had brought along a fine collection of records, seventy-eights in those days, which included dance bands and vocalist favourites. We listened to Ambrose, Roy Fox, Benny Goodman, Duke Ellington, Artie Shaw and Lew Stone; vocalists, Sam Browne, Bing Crosby and Al Bowlly, killed in an air-raid in 1941. But the favourite by unanimous decision was 'Begin the Beguine' played by Joe Loss and his orchestra and sung by Chick Henderson who, later in the war, was lost at sea. We even preferred this record to the original Artie Shaw version and we just about flogged it to death. Whoever visited us had 'Begin the Beguine' poured into their earholes. We used to sing with much gusto but with little melody, 'South of the Border', the 'Beer Barrel Polka', 'Deep Purple', 'A Tisket, a Tasket' and 'Little Sir Echo'. Those neighbours who were still around used to complain, justifiably, of our rendering of 'Little Sir Echo'. It did sound awful, I suppose, but we were enthusiastic about our version of 'Beer Barrel Polka'. I had heard the tune in Belgium a few weeks before the outbreak of war. It seemed to suit the times.

I had met bandleaders Duke Ellington and Cab Calloway through my father, when I was a child, but my interest in bands never did amount to much. Our expert on contemporary band music was Harold, who wrote song lyrics and showed promise as a song writer. While serving in the R.A.F. he transferred to the entertainment section and found himself concerned with entertainers from the U.S.A. who were visiting various theatres of war to entertain the Services. After the war he continued in show business, representing such stars as Ella Fitzgerald and Frank Sinatra in Britain and became a leading impresario.

Sometimes when cooking became too much for us or when we just could not face another can of baked beans, my girlfriend came and helped us out. She could grill such steaks as were still available and fortunately, she too liked 'Begin the Beguine', although as far as bands were concerned, she preferred Jack Payne, Jack Hylton and Paul Whiteman.

We had met only a month before at the Hammersmith Palais where I danced all over her feet to the music of Oscar Rabin and his band – or it could have been Joe Loss. I was not paying much attention to the music at the time; not that I ever did pay much attention to the music while dancing as it invariably interfered with my timing. We were married a year later when I came home on a forty-eight hour furlough from the army. I did not think that was sufficient so I overstayed my leave by seven weeks and thought it well worth the consequences I suffered. When I went back to rejoin my unit I remember humming 'Roll Out the Barrel'. I had no qualms. At the time I thought life was too short to worry.

Henry Hall visits the circus. He is seen with flying trapeze artist Miss Concello and Bertram Mills in 1935.

Opposite above, Paul Whiteman appears in a film; *below*, Louis Armstrong and his band.

At the beginning of the thirties, Jack Hylton was already established as a bandleader, and his band, thought by many to be the leading European show band of the decade, made extensive tours of the continent covering thousands of miles. At a time when the B.B.C. paid the staff of its London Orchestra on a scale ranging from a minimum of eleven pounds per week, Jack was paying his men top salaries and none of them earned less than forty pounds per week; some were paid sixty. They were paid extra for additional shows. But the work of a bandsman was the hardest and most hectic in the music profession. In London he might be expected to start a recording session at 9 a.m. and continue until an hour before a matinee performance, say at the London Palladium. The band would play the first house, then a special coach took the musicians to, perhaps, the Finsbury Park Empire to play the first house there. Then back they would go to the Palladium for the second house, returning again to the Finsbury Empire to play the second house. After that they might be rushed to a dance hall such as the Twickenham Lido where they played until three in the morning.

Doing one night stands on the continent, bandsmen might not know until the last minute whether they would be playing Brussels or Amsterdam. Life was a sequence of trains, taxis and charabancs with little time to spare for even a haircut. One of Jack's musicians would cut hair on a train. Yet on the stage the musicians sparkled clean and debonair, showing few signs of their arduous journeys.

Once while performing in Nottingham, Jack received a cable with an offer of a large sum of money to broadcast to New York from London that same evening. The band boarded a charabanc and were rushed to London arriving just ten minutes before it was time to go on the air. The band played a half hour session and was hurried back to Nottingham immediately. And that was before motorways.

Jack Hylton and his band were well known to radio listeners all over the country and Jack also presented radio programmes in France, Czechoslovakia and Austria. Jack's was the first British band to broadcast direct to the United States and in the following year, 1932, whilst touring Europe, he was prepared to play in the U.S.S.R., but was refused an entry permit at the last moment.

Hylton's approach to music was to try to achieve a balance of rhythm, melody and harmony to form what he called 'symphonic syncopation'. Whatever he called it, he managed to introduce a subtle touch which appealed to the British public in particular, and also to many other Europeans, who appreciated its 'Britishness'. However, there were some who found his arrangements sterile and his selections somewhat jumbled. His repertoire included popular music, hit songs, light classics, and an occasional more ambitious item. Once at a concert at the Opera House in Paris he played excerpts from Stravinsky's opera, 'Maura', while the great composer was present, a pointer to Hylton's confidence. There was an underlying staidness to Hylton's music, yet he did not ignore the use of the jazz idiom. It was Hylton, after all, who arranged the successful tour of Duke Ellington in Britain, although this could have been Jack Hylton wearing his impresario hat. He did employ jazz musicians, but there again, whether it was because of a genuine feeling for jazz music or a recognition of its particular popularity at the time is something that has never been resolved.

Records made by Hylton and his band were generally popular. Until the autumn of 1931 when he went over to Decca, he had recorded for H.M.V., and he returned to them in 1935. Successful numbers of Jack Hylton's band included Billy Ternent's arrangement of 'Limehouse Blues' and 'Tiger Rag'. Popular songs of 1932 included 'Auf Wiedersehn My Dear', 'Love is the Sweetest Thing' and 'Goodnight Vienna'. Of course, most bands were recording popular songs of the period among which there were many novelty and comic pieces such as 'Minnie the Moocher', 'Ain't it Grand to be Bloomin' Well Dead' and 'He's Dead But He Won't Lie Down', but Jack Hylton preferred to play melodic numbers, though there was no doubt about his versatility and musicianship.

In 1934, Jack presented a special programme at the old Holborn Empire to celebrate the tenth anniversary of the inauguration of his band. It was the year of 'Miss Otis Regrets', 'Smoke Gets in Your Eyes', 'The Continental' and 'Winter Wonderland' and the year when Gracie Fields first sang 'Isle of Capri' and 'Sing as We Go'.

In 1935 when Jack was reputed to be one of the highest paid band-

The rendezvous of the musical profession, London's Archer Street in 1935.

Chick Henderson and *far right* Louis Armstrong.

Chick Henderson and *far right* Louis Armstrong.

leaders in Britain, he took his band on a fourteenth tour of Europe which included a visit to Germany at a time when the Nazis were becoming increasingly unpopular with many Britons and Americans. In the autumn when Jack turned up in the United States for a series of engagements, the band was banned by the American Federation of Musicians and had to return to Britain. Undeterred, Hylton stayed behind with his arrangers, Billy Ternent and Melle Weersma, Alec Templeton and vocalists Eve Beck, Peggy Dell and Pat O'Malley. With a band composed of American musicians, he was able to under-take regular broadcasts and fulfil hotel and theatre engagements. He had a good reception everywhere. It was the year of 'Red Sails in the Sunset', 'Cheek to Cheek' and 'You are my Lucky Star'. Jack returned to England just as the Spanish Civil War began in July 1936 to form a new band. Songs of that period broadcast over and over again included 'These Foolish Things', 'It's a Sin to Tell a Lie' and 'The Way You Look Tonight'.

For the next two years Jack was busy in Britain and it was not until 1938 that he went off on another continental tour – the last one he made. It was the year of 'Music, Maestro, Please', 'In the Still of the Night' and 'Thanks for the Memory'. It was also the year of Munich.

In 1939 Jack Hylton and his band were featured in the film *The Band Wagon* and after the war broke out, Jack went on to make frequent broadcasts. From 'Deep Purple' and 'Begin the Beguine', it became 'We're Gonna Hang out the Washing on the Siegfried Line',

80

'Wish me Luck as You Wave me Goodbye', 'Run, Rabbit, Run' and 'There'll Always be an England'. Hylton was approaching the end of his bandleader era and beginning his mighty reign as an impresario.

The other famous Jack of the period was Jack Payne and in the world of variety and show business he was Jack Hylton's only real rival. Jack Payne, while serving in the Royal Flying Corps in World War One, had organised a dance band to entertain his fellow airmen and after the war he took up dance band music as a career. For a number of years he travelled around with various groups of half a dozen or more musicians and in 1925 he was fortunate to secure an engagement for a few months at the Hotel Cecil in the Strand. Soon the B.B.C. was relaying his music from the hotel.

In February 1928 he was appointed Director of Dance Music by the B.B.C. and by the beginning of the thirties he was broadcasting seven days a week and recording for Columbia and Regal as well as appearing on the stage. Among his leading musicians at the time were trumpeter Jack Jackson (who later had his own band,) multi-reed man E. O. 'Poggy' Pogson and violinist Eric Siday. Jack Payne's signature tune, 'Say it with Music', was one of the best known in the thirties.

In 1932, Jack Payne left the B.B.C., taking the orchestra, which was under contract to him, on tour. But ten of the musicians decided to break away after a wrangle with Jack, and form their own group. This led to some further acrimony when the group calling itself the Barnstormers advertised itself as 'Pleasure Without Payne' and promptly had an injunction slapped on it, forbidding the use of the ambiguous description.

Payne lost no time in finding replacements for the recalcitrant musicians and continued to appear on the stage and to make recordings. He recorded for Rex and the Crystalate Recording Company, most of his recordings being medleys from musical shows, contemporary popular songs and comedy numbers such as 'My Brother Makes the Noises for the Talkies'. Today some of the material would seem to be lacking in musical merit but at the time, Jack Payne was immensely popular on stage, radio and gramophone.

He made several successful tours including one in 1936 to South Africa where his chief vocalist, Billy Scott Coomber, pitched in with a few choruses in Afrikaans for the benefit of the locals. Not long afterwards, Jack announced that he was retiring from the stage to take up farming in Buckinghamshire, but he did continue continental broadcasts and made a number of appearances at Sunday concerts. Also, as an impresario, he controlled a number of road shows.

At the beginning of 1938, Jack was back on tour with a twenty-piece band in a show called 'Round the Dial'. Just over a year later he disbanded again, but as war approached he formed a new band. On Christmas day, 1939, he was in France, the first bandleader to take out a band to play for the Forces. The soldiers joined in the choruses of

'We're Going to Hang out our Washing on the Siegfried Line' and the 'Beer Barrel Polka'.

One of the most illustrious names in the history of British dance band music, Ambrose was already a household word by the beginning of the thirties and to prove it, Ambrose had bought himself a brand new Speed-Six Bentley.

He had started his career as a violinist in a cinema orchestra in New York and by the age of twenty he was musical director of a club in the Palais Royal, New York. In 1927 he came to London to become the musical director at the Mayfair Hotel and not long afterwards he was offered a recording contract by Brunswick. He also made records for the Gramophone Company, now E.M.I., but complained that he found it constricting. In 1928 he started his radio career with broadcasts from the Mayfair Hotel at regular intervals, except for a short period in 1929 when the hotel was in dispute with the B.B.C. over the Corporation's ban on those announcements and vocal choruses which could be construed as plugging. He resumed his broadcasts at the optimal time of 10.30 p.m. until midnight on Saturdays, and this, together with his records, consolidated his position in the world of dance band music for the next decade.

From 1933 until almost the end of 1936, Ambrose was at the Embassy Club; he then returned to the Mayfair Hotel. In 1937 he went into partnership with bandleader Jack Harris, taking over the management of Ciro's Club. His band was more popular than ever with such numbers as 'These Foolish Things', 'It's a Sin to Tell a Lie', 'The Way You Look Tonight' and 'The Touch of Your Lips'. However his honeymoon with Jack Harris at Ciro's was soon over; Ambrose quit and disbanded.

In the spring of 1938 Ambrose and his band were playing at the Café de Paris in Piccadilly, where, three years later, bandleader Snake Hips Johnson was killed when a bomb struck the crowded café at the height of an air raid. In the period 1938–9 the Ambrose orchestra was rarely heard, although in August 1938 the full orchestra made a successful two months tour. Once more, however, the full band was discontinued and an octet went on tour with Denny Denis, Les Carew, Vera Lynn, Maxie Bacon and Evelyn Dall. Drummer Maxie Bacon had become extremely popular with his comedy songs such as 'The Flat Foot Floogie', 'Bei Mir Bist du Schön', 'The Donkey Serenade' and 'Music, Maestro, Please'.

Ambrose returned to the air in 1939 with a pick-up unit when the B.B.C., who had previously claimed that they could not afford his services, dug deeper into their pockets. Three months after the outbreak of war, Ambrose was back at the Mayfair Hotel leading a resident band which included George Chisholm, Billy Amstell and Stanley Black, but this was the last outstanding band he was to lead. The exigencies of war soon made inroads on his talented personnel, many of them leaving to go into the R.A.F.

Except for the twelve months from autumn 1937, when he refused to renew his contract because the company wanted to cut his fees, Ambrose recorded with Decca from 1934 to 1949. As early as 1932 he had sixty-two records released in one year.

The musicianship of Bert Ambrose was of the highest standard. He maintained strict discipline over his bandsmen and was uncompromising in his attitude towards outside engagements by his musicians without his permission. He insisted on impeccable interpretation of his musical ideas and this sometimes resulted in a stereotyped background to his music. Ambrose was always aware of the constraints imposed by the musical taste of the clientele of hotels and clubs where he played – as well as by the acoustics and atmosphere. Nevertheless, the high standard of his music rarely faltered and he performed with distinction at Buckingham Palace and Windsor on many occasions.

Born in Denver, Colorado, Roy Fox was only a few months old when

Lew Stone and his band, 1933.

his parents moved to Hollywood. By the age of sixteen he was a professional musician in Santa Monica and before long was working for Abe Lyman. Roy led a band for the first time when he was nineteen, at the Club Royale in Culver City and thereafter served resident engagements in Los Angeles, Miami and New York.

While on a location job in Hollywood he was offered a job as musical director by Fox Studios and while working for them he received a request from London to play an eight week engagement at the Café de Paris, London.

Then in May 1931, he became resident bandleader at the brand new Monseigneur restaurant where, with such outstanding musicians as trumpeter-vocalist Nat Gonella, Sid Buckman, Joe Ferrie, the Amstells, Lew Stone and vocalist Al Bowlly, his orchestra was an immediate success and the B.B.C. was quick to secure it for a weekly broadcast. Soon Roy's signature tune, 'Whispering', was known throughout Britain. Unfortunately, Roy was taken severely ill about five months later and had to spend some time in hospital. The leadership of the band was taken over by Lew Stone. Roy returned to take charge of the band again but a year later, in October 1932, by mutual agreement with the management, he left the Monseigneur and Lew Stone took over the band again.

Roy Fox, with a newly formed band, opened at the Café Anglais in London's Leicester Square but a few months later in January 1933, having been released from his contract, he moved to the Kit Kat Club. A year later he was at the Café de Paris for a few months before going on a nationwide theatre tour. Whilst touring the provinces he fitted in broadcasts for local studios and recording sessions for home and overseas, as well as managing to appear in a film called *Radio Pirates*. This hectic way of life was to continue until the break up of the band in 1938. Roy's health suffered and he went to Australia to recuperate. With the outbreak of war in 1939 he was unable to return to Britain and he stayed there for the duration.

Roy Fox made many recordings for Decca and H.M.V. The 1932 version of 'Georgia on my Mind', featuring Nat Gonella, was a particular favourite and no bottle party could be complete without it. Other favourites were, 'How am I doin' heh-heh', 'The Old Man of the Mountains' and 'You're my Everything' with vocalist Al Bowlly. Another of Roy's popular vocalists was Denny Dennis whose style in numbers such as 'June in January' and 'Everything I Have is Yours' fitted into the sophisticated smoothness and quiet rhythm of Roy Fox's band. Other well-remembered numbers of the band are 'Pennies from Heaven' and 'September in the Rain'.

In September 1930, at the age of twenty, the incredible Joe Loss was leading a seven-piece band at the famous Astoria Ballroom in Charing Cross Road, London – in those days, the popular rendezvous of dancing couples. Joe Loss and the other Astoria bandleader, Oscar Rabin, with his Romany Dance Band, played the kind of music that appealed to all who liked dancing. They came flocking to the Astoria from all over London.

Joe, who came from the East End of London, studied music at the Trinity College of Music and the London School of Music. He started as a professional violinist playing in various bands until going to the Astoria. In 1931 he moved to the Kit Kat Club as resident bandleader, staying until 1933, the year he made his first broadcast. Having started in variety while still at the Kit Kat, Joe topped the bill at the old Holborn Empire early in 1934. Later that year he returned to the Astoria to lead a twelve-piece band and once again he was eagerly welcomed by thousands of young dancers.

He made frequent broadcasts and recordings and went on an annual tour to show himself to his fans up and down the country. Everywhere he was enthusiastically received. His vocalists, Chick Henderson, Monte Rey and Marjorie Kingsley, were great favourites, especially Chick Henderson. At one time Adelaide Hall featured as one of Joe's singers.

The war started in 1939 while Joe was on a summer tour. He returned to the Astoria for a while but early in 1940, after playing for the British Expeditionary Force, he left the Astoria to take up extensive tours of the country. Joe's music has always shown the quality produced by his early musical training. His music was true dance music. Even novices on the dance floor were able to respond to his easy rhythm. Joe has always preferred playing in dance halls rather than in hotels and restaurants. Hotels are for sleeping; restaurants are for eating; dance halls are for dancing. That sounds right. Joe's signature tune, 'In the Mood', was well chosen.

Ray Noble's band was essentially a studio band although he did tour as a showband on occasions and, in fact, toured Britain in 1938, ostensibly as leader of Jimmy Trump Davidson's band from Canada. This tour included two weeks at the London Palladium.

Ray Noble's tremendous reputation was based on his prodigious output of records, his song writing and his skilful arrangements. He composed famous hits of the thirties such as 'Goodnight Sweetheart', 'Love is the Sweetest Thing', 'By the Fireside', 'The Very Thought of You' and the evergreen 'Cherokee'.

Ray, born in Brighton, started playing piano at the age of ten and soon became interested in dance music. In 1927 he won a 'Melody Maker' contest for arrangers and before long he was working for Laurence Wright, music publishers, as a staff manager In 1928 he was working with Jack Payne at the B.B.C. when Carrol Gibbons, director of house bands at H.M.V. was contracted by M.G.M. in America and he suggested that Noble replace him. Ray, eminently suitable for the role, took over from Carrol in the middle of 1929.

At the start of the thirties, Ray was well established in the recording field but little known to the general public. He was inhibited at H.M.V. by the fact that he was always left with the less commercial titles after Jack Hylton and Ambrose had had their pick. Furthermore, he was not given any special billing – his records were released under the name of the New Mayfair Orchestra or the New Mayfair Novelty Orchestra. However the success of his records led to subsequent releases under his own name – Ray Noble and his Orchestra. These records included 'Close Your Eyes', 'Here Lies Love' and 'Lazy Day' which featured vocals by Al Bowlly. His musicians included Nat Gonella, Freddy Gardiner and, as well as Al Bowlly, his vocalists included Val Rosing, Sam Browne and Elsie Carlisle. His records were extremely popular in the U.S.A. as well as in Britain, and in 1934 Ray went to America, taking Al Bowlly with him.

Ray's first band in the U.S.A. was organised for him by Glenn Miller who was a great admirer of Ray's work. Ray became busier than ever and his recordings were competent if not stunning in their general impact. Nevertheless, his records continued in popularity and when he moved to Los Angeles in 1939 it was not long before he became successful as a radio personality as well as a bandleader.

Hard-working Lew Stone started his musical career playing in a small London night club. Then, as pianist in Bert Ralton's band, he made a tour of South Africa and on his return, played for a while with Bert Ambrose. He started riding high when he replaced Roy Fox as bandleader at the Monseigneur in October 1932 and became an immediate success. His broadcasts, versatile and with high musical and programme content, together with skilful presentation, became the special delight for thousands of listeners all over Britain on Tuesdays between 10.30 p.m. and midnight.

While based at the Monseigneur, until leaving at the end of 1933, Lew often doubled at variety theatres. As musical director for British and Dominion Films from late 1931 to 1935, he was also engaged in producing music for dozens of films and he and his band were featured in some of them. Such well known musicians as trumpeter Nat Gonella, bassist Tiny Winters and vocalist Al Bowlly were helped in building their reputation by appearing with Lew Stone.

Towards the end of 1933 Lew went over to the Café Anglais, but four months later he was back at the Monseigneur, where he stayed until it closed in the summer to make way for a new cinema. After a provincial tour, Lew opened at the Hollywood Restaurant following this with an extensive theatre tour which went on into 1936. Then, with a smaller band, he took up residence in the Café de Paris.

In 1937 Lew was musical director for the Rodgers and Hart musical, *On Your Toes*, which opened in London in February 1937, and he left the Café de Paris in July of the year. In the following year he was engaged mainly as musical director on film work for the British National company and on the stage show *Hide and Seek*, starring Bobby Howes and Cicely Courtneidge. However he did not neglect broadcasting and using pick-up groups he was brilliantly successful, winning acclaim from critics and public alike. However, he was back in the field in 1938, being one of those chosen by Billy Butlin to lead a band for the opening of a new holiday camp at Clacton, followed by playing a week at Skegness.

Then in September 1938, Lew, with a nine-piece band was back at the Café de Paris, broadcasting frequently in the months that followed. In October he undertook the job of musical director to the show *Under Your Hat*, which starred Jack Buchanan and this carried him through the fateful year of 1939.

Lew Stone started recording regularly as early as 1929 with Duophone. He made some good records for Regal-Zonophone before moving to Decca. In all his recordings, which included hot jazz, sentimental ballads and comedy numbers, Lew's treatment of subject was always apt. His versions of a particular composition of any type seemed somehow to be more sympathetically, precisely and harmoniously performed than by other contemporary bands. His Gene Gifford numbers for the Casa Loma Orchestra are remembered today for their ensemble precision and individual musical skill, as are his orchestral versions of Forsythe's compositions. Stone's recordings were particularly successful with vocals by Al Bowlly. His arrangements were especially sensitive and evocative, attuned to the quality of the number recorded and the tone of the vocalist.

Playing in plush nightclubs and small hotels, watching the rich gorge and guzzle champagne like water, Lew was always conscious of the vast gap between the rich and the poor. He was grateful for his success and modest about his ability. Unlike many other bandleaders of the period he did not let success go to his head and never lost sight of the fact that he was working for a living. He worked hard at his job, sometimes sixteen hours or more a day, and his achievements in the realm of British dance music made a lasting impression.

Artie Shaw was born in New York's Lower East Side, the son of a Jewish tailor. His early jobs were mainly with travelling bands, but after a while he moved on to freelancing in New York and in the early

Outside the Monseigneur in 1932 and *far right* Artie Shaw.

thirties played in studio saxophone sections and was alternative first choice for any clarinet assignment. Often with him, playing a similar role, would be Benny Goodman.

Artie had no great desire to lead a band. He was interested more in being an innovator than a musician. However, in May 1935, he had an offer to play at a jazz concert, one of the first of its kind, at the Imperial Theatre, New York, and he decided on a bold experiment. He wanted to produce something that would sound different from other bands and combos on the programme and so he wrote a piece for clarinet and string quartet which he called 'Interlude in B Flat'. He then added guitar, bass and drums to put it into the jazz context.

Artie's piece was the hit of the show and he was pressed from all sides to form a band of his own. Despite his reluctance, Artie saw a means of accumulating the large sums of money that would allow him to quit the music business and make, as he put it, 'some altogether different life for myself'.

Benny Goodman in his heyday.

The band Artie created was different in composition and sound from the swing bands then in vogue but it was impossible to beat the tide and he found himself drowning in the flood of swing. Artie said that everybody liked the band except the audience, so after less than two years he was forced to yield to the inevitable. He formed a band with standard instrumentation to sail along like so many other bandleaders in the wake of Benny Goodman, King of Swing.

However, as Artie's band was swinging along during a long run at the Roseland State Ballroom, Boston, Mass., Artie's interest began to concentrate on the music of Cole Porter, Jerome Kern, Richard Rodgers and other composers whose melodic compositions sweetened the musical theatre in the twenties and thirties. Artie's arrangement of Cole Porter's 'Begin the Beguine', recorded and released in 1938, was a phenomenal success. Artie was immediately swept on to the crest of the wave, superseding his rival, Benny Goodman.

The following year he worked ceaselessly. Shaw's 'Nightmare', 'Frenesi', 'Concerto for Clarinet' and other recordings were played the world over. But the pace was hot. Twice in 1939 Artie collapsed on the bandstand, completely exhausted as the jitterbugs stamped and yelled for him to play. He was in hospital for six weeks suffering from a severe blood disorder. He felt that he was unable to go on with his music and in December 1939 he left his band and went to Mexico. Referring to that time, Artie said, 'I wanted to resign from the planet, not just from music'.

By 1935, Benny Goodman had put in ten years of hard slogging as a professional musician in Chicago and New York, travelling with Ben Pollack's band and freelancing on New York's radio stations. His first break came when he was contracted as one of three regular bands on a coast-to-coast broadcast sponsored by the National Biscuit Company. The show was called *Let's Dance* and one of the other bands was Xavier Cugat's Latin American group. Benny said, 'At that time we were playing for biscuits and picked up a few crumbs'.

But 21 August 1935 was Benny's real red-letter day. That was the day when, without realising it, he opened what was to be known as the Great Swing Era. Goodman and his band had arrived in Los Angeles after criss-crossing the U.S.A. in a series of one night stands. The band was way down in the dumps. Nothing they had played seemed to please the patrons. The manager of a ballroom in Denver complained to Goodman's booking agent, stating that for his money, Goodman's music was lousy and the leader was a pain in the ass.

The last booking on this miserable tour was at the Palomar Ballroom, Los Angeles, and by that time Benny was very worried about the chances of his band keeping together. It surprised him to find the dance hall packed and after his recent experiences on the road he opened nervously with the usual routine of popular tune arrangements. His efforts were coldly received by the crowd and Benny's heart sank.

Benny Goodman, playing on.

'What the hell!' he thought. 'If we're going out, we might as well go out playing the music we like for a change, instead of trying to please the crowd with old pot-boilers.' So Benny produced some arrangements scored by the redoubtable Fletcher Henderson and let himself and his band go with 'Sugar Foot Stomp'. Bunny Berrigan took a trumpet solo and really put his lips to it, standing over the crowd as it swayed toward the dais in a sudden ecstasy of excitement, the music snapping electrically about the ears and tingling all the way down to their feet.

By the time the band played 'King Porter Stomp' and 'Sometimes I'm Happy' the youngsters were thronging the bandstand, cheering and stomping, and that *was* music to the ears of Benny and his revitalised boys. The Swing Era had arrived to make Benny and his band the biggest attraction in the U.S.A. and to launch some of Goodman's sidemen, such as Gene Krupa, Lionel Hampton and Harry James, into careers of unprecedented fame.

In March 1937 when the band was due to open at the Paramount Theatre, New York City – the Mecca of all big bands – the streets were teeming with teenagers who had played hookey from school to see the morning show. Over twenty-one thousand people passed in and out of the theatre, the kids packing the aisles, climbing over seats and charging the squads of stewards in an effort to get to the band. The fans yelled, cheered, sighed and cried in a frenzy of ecstasy.

In the following January, the Goodman orchestra gave a jazz concert in Carnegie Hall; it was the first dance orchestra ever to do so. For this great occasion, Benny supplemented his team with men from the orchestras of Count Basie and Duke Ellington. The show was completely sold out and the enraptured audience rocked the theatre with their foot-stamping exuberance and exulting cries of pleasure. Jazz had become big time. Yet Benny had his doubts about the concert aspect of the business. His preference was playing music for dancers. However, he had to admit later that he was trapped in the concert business.

By 1930 Duke Ellington was already a seasoned performer. In 1923 he had been playing at the Kentucky Club in midtown Manhattan and although the band broadcast nightly at 2 a.m. on a local station, it was hardly the high spot for a show. However, it so happened that one evening the well known Chicago band of King Oliver, due to open at the famous Harlem night spot, the Cotton Club, failed to put in an appearance. This was mainly due to the failure of the management to cough up the amount of money demanded by Oliver. The Cotton Club was forced to look elsewhere in a hurry. It looked as far as the Kentucky Club, but as Ellington and his band were already booked to play a two week engagement in Philadelphia, it was necessary for friends of the Cotton Club's management to indulge in a little skulduggery to free Ellington from his commitment.

The elegant Duke Ellington.

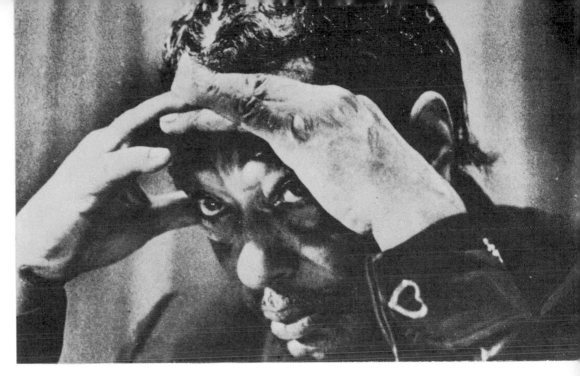

So Duke Ellington made his debut at the Cotton Club, starting a five year run that was to bring him to the forefront of popular American bands. Moreover, working for the Columbia Broadcasting System several times a week brought Duke and his band international fame. At the time, the Cotton Club was patronised exclusively by whites seeking novelty, thrills and excitement. The management cynically catered for them by providing an atmosphere, a style of music and a floor show that reeked of the jungle. This was what effcte, white clientele expected to see in Harlem, and it brought them flocking.

It was what was called the jungle period of Ellington, when he featured many of his own compositions such as 'Black and Tan Fantasy', but there was really nothing cynical about Duke's approach to music and the playing of his band. His music had infinite quality, rhythm and style, and the clientele of the Cotton Club probably got a good deal more than it deserved. Ellington's music evolved into the lyricism of 'Creole Love Call', the haunting 'Mood Indigo' and the melodic 'Solitude', 'Sophisticated Lady' and 'I Let a Song go Out of my Heart'.

Ellington was always highly regarded by musicians as well as by everyone who ever listened to him. He was popular with his fellow men and he retained his musicians for longer periods than most other bands. His bandsmen were essentially loyal to him. One baritone saxophonist, Harry Carney, joined Duke in 1926 and stayed with him for almost fifty years.

Ellington's band was a large jazz unit of unique style and quality, rating high with other elite black bands such as McKinney's Cotton Pickers, Fletcher Henderson's, Luis Russell's, Bennie Moten's and Cab Calloway's. Duke's elegance, insouciance and confident style captivated the public throughout the thirties and continued to do so into the present decade. His personality, flair and own special magic, known throughout the world, still survive him today.

91

Public enemy

Above, Clyde Barrow; *below*,
Ray Hamilton.

*You must understand man as he is and not demand of his
nature something it does not possess.*

Sergey Timoveyovich Aksakov (1791–1859) to Gogol.

FROM THE MIDDLE TWENTIES THROUGH THE THIRTIES UNTIL
the outbreak of war, my father used to receive regularly tabloid
newspapers from New York and I always found them fascinating
reading. They presented a new, exciting world with their box-car
headlines, slick, punchy turns of phrase, candid pictures and revealing
advertisements. There never seemed to be a shortage of killings to
dominate the front page. The Americans used the word 'slaying' for
killing or murder in those days. I well remember a headline that took
up the whole front page of a New York daily, 'Diamond Slain'.

I read about bootleggers, gangsters, bank robbers and more or less
mundane murderers such as Judd Gray and Ruth Snyder. I was
familiar with Capone, Jack Diamond, Dutch Schultz and Albert
Anastasia. I remember going to school with a copy of a New York
newspaper in my satchel to show my friends, announcing the gangland
slaying of Chicago gangster, Joe Aiello. I remember reading about
Bonnie Parker and Clyde Barrow when they murdered Deputy
Malcolm Davis in 1933 and again when they themselves were slain in
1934. I read about bank robber 'Pretty Boy' Floyd, 'Babyface' Nelson,
Vernon Miller, Frank Nash, Raymond Hamilton and the murderous
Ma Barker and her psychopathic sons; about the unspeakable Alvin
Karpis, ruthless killer, kidnapper and bank robber, and dozens of
others.

But of all the criminals who hogged the headlines of the newspapers
in the early thirties, John Dillinger stands out as the personification of
gangsterdom in the U.S.A. Yet Dillinger, puffed up by the press and
portrayed as a latter-day Jesse James, or Wild Bill Hickok, was
described years later as dull-witted and incompetent as a criminal and
as a gangleader. This was not quite so, but he was a posturing braggart

John Dillinger in 1934, with *above* his farmer father and *right* Main Street, Mooresville, Indiana, his home town.

93

with a homicidal streak whom the press, for reasons of their own, built up into an international figure by exaggerating the success of his criminal exploits. The fact was that Dillinger's associates were all notorious robbers and killers, and by placing Dillinger at the top of the heap, the press created solid copy that was guaranteed to satisfy the public with the vicarious thrills that it craved.

When Dillinger, at the age of thirty-one, was finally shot dead by detectives in 1934, he was the official Public Enemy Number One – a sort of top of the pops in the criminal charts of those days. The sensational news of his demise and details of his career appeared in newspapers all over the world. Some newspapers suggested that he had not been given a fair chance and that he had been shot down like a mad dog.

I kept the New York papers proclaiming the death of Dillinger, together with the hundreds of other newspapers with spectacular headlines that I used to collect. Unfortunately, my mother handed them all over for paper salvage half way through World War Two while I was overseas. However, I still have a magazine published in May 1934 in which an article about John Dillinger appeared two months before his death. It summed up his sordid career by stating that he had had a misplaced ingenuity, a grim sense of humour and a perverted valour. I suppose the same could be said of Hitler, Mussolini and Franco, as well as of other notorious gangsters.

In May 1933 John Herman Dillinger was paroled from the Michigan State Penitentiary after having served nearly nine of a fourteen year sentence for assault and battery with intent to rob. He was of medium height, had receding hair, a boot nose, a cleft chin and unyielding glassy brown eyes which gave him the nickname, Snake Eyes. He walked with a slight limp from having poured hot metal in the heel of his shoe while working in the prison foundry in order to make it easier for him to malinger.

A mere boy when he had first entered prison, Dillinger found himself a grown man in the hard world of the great depression when he came out; a world where millions of unemployed were scrabbling for a living, where most could barely keep their heads above water, where thousands of firms had been forced out of business and where bootlegging czars were the nouveau-riche.

Dillinger was ill-equipped to find a slot in the new society. He had no real education or trade, was out of touch with the legitimate ways of life and he certainly was not prepared to become a wage slave, even were it possible to get a job. But he did have some assets that could serve him in good stead in the illegitimate ways of life. He had learned a good deal of criminal know-how in prison, as well as acquiring a few

potentially useful criminal friends and contacts. So it was not long before Dillinger threw in his lot with a small group of desperadoes in the hold-up business.

In one particular roadhouse hold-up Dillinger gratuitously slugged a customer in passing. It was symptomatic of his hostility to the general public and he demonstrated this again a month after leaving prison when, in an abortive raid on a factory, he shot the manager in the leg. He seemed to find this incident exhilarating. Three weeks later, on 10 July, Dillinger and two associates, William Shaw and Paul 'Lefty' Parker, held up a bank in Ohio and got away with a sizeable sum of money. Dillinger was beginning to feel that he was 'up and coming' in his profession. On 16 July the gang ran into a police trap and Shaw and Parker were arrested. Dillinger and another associate, Harry Copeland, managed to get away in another car and the very next day were back in business with a new recruit, a hoodlum called Noble Claycomb. They held up a bank in Daleville, Indiana, but the pickings were poor and Dillinger was beginning to feel frustrated. However the exploit did earn him some notoriety. When it was reported that he had vaulted the counter at the bank, the newspapers referred to him as the 'athletic bandit'. Dillinger liked that. Claycomb did not. He was soon caught and he implicated his partners, including Dillinger.

On 4 August Dillinger and Copeland struck again. They held up a bank in Montipelier, Indiana, and made a clean getaway – ten thousand dollars richer. Dillinger felt smug. Things were looking up and there were dozens of banks he felt he could draw on at any time. However, Dillinger's exploits had attracted the attention of Matt Leach of the Indiana State Police. He was to become Dillinger's implacable enemy, but blissfully unaware of this and contemptuous of lawmen in any case, Dillinger continued his depredations.

On 14 August 1933, he and Copeland sauntered into the Citizens National Bank, Bluffton, Ohio, while three of their associates waited casually outside. Dillinger and Copeland had only managed to grab a paltry two thousand dollars when the alarm bell suddenly sounded. The shaken gangsters fled precipitately, firing indiscriminately at all and sundry.

Undeterred, Dillinger picked his next target, a bank in Indianapolis. This time with two more 'hoods', he robbed the bank of twenty-four thousand dollars. Eyewitnesses identified Dillinger who, once again, had drawn attention to himself by vaulting the counter.

Since leaving prison, Dillinger had been nursing a plan to help friends that were still inside to escape. Now with plenty of cash to back his plan, he set about carrying it out and there is no doubt that he did a very competent job in this instance. He made arrangements for guns to be smuggled in to his comrades and for a Mary Kinder in Michigan City to supply clothes and refuge for the escapees. Having set the operation in motion, Dillinger found time to relax. Unfortunately for him, he chose to relax with a married woman, a sister of one of the convicts, in a rooming house in Dayton which, at that time, was under surveillance by detectives.

When police burst into the apartment they caught Dillinger with his trousers down, so to speak, and his pistol harmless on a table. It was a very chagrined Dillinger who was hauled off to the Montgomery County Jail. That was on the evening of 22 September 1933. On 26 September the Dillinger plan found fruition. Ten dangerous criminals, all convicted bank-robbers and murderers, escaped from Michigan State Penitentiary. They were Russell Clark, Harry Pierpont, John Hamilton, Charles Makeley, James Jenkins, Edward Shouse, Joseph Fox, Joseph Burns, Walter Dietrich and James Clark (no relation to Russell Clark).

James Clark was soon caught and James Jenkins was killed in a shoot-out with the police. The others managed to reach Kinder's hide-out where they soon brazenly established themselves with girl friends and proceeded to make up for the time they had spent in prison.

FREE PATTERN and NOVELTY GIFT NEXT WEEK !

WOMAN'S PICTORIAL

3^d

ol. 23. No. 576.   JANUARY 23rd, 1932.   Every Monday.

"OVER THE HEATH."   *From the painting by DOROTHEA SHARPE.*

NEXT WEEK—The Beginning of a Brilliant New Novel

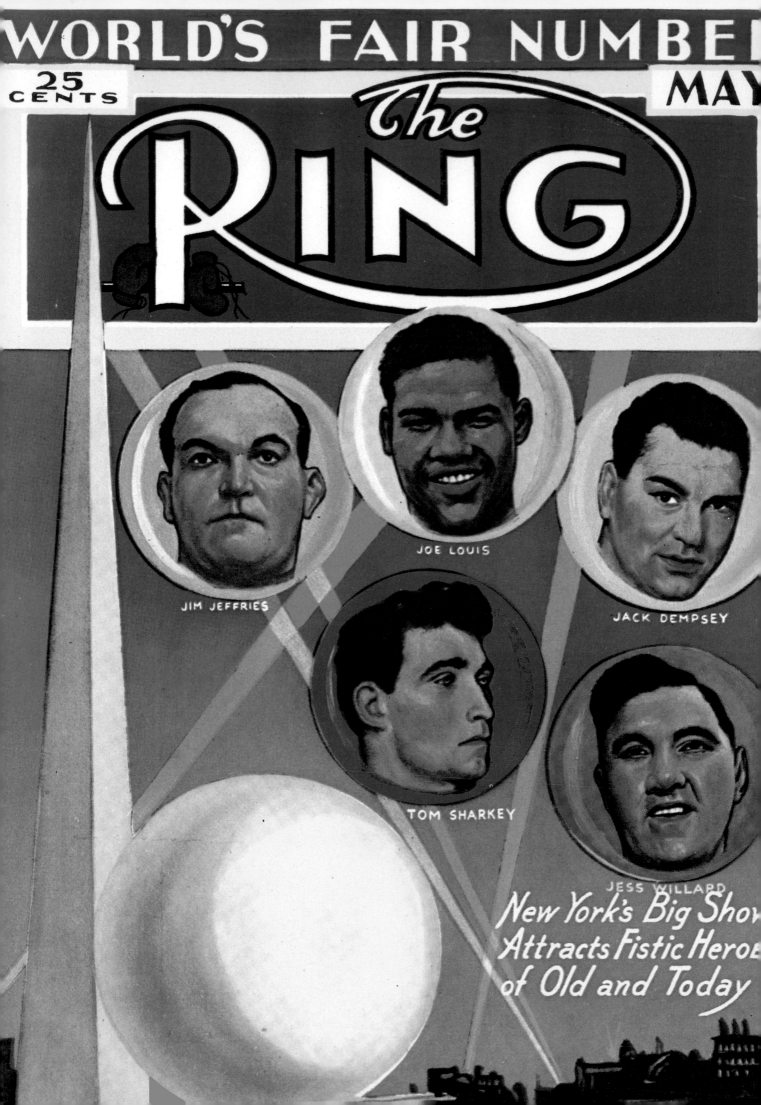

An American cinema 'lobby
still' of the 1930s.

GUINNESS FOR STRENGTH

Cigarette picture cards issued in 1935 to commemorate the Silver Jubilee of King George V's accession to the throne (1910).

WILLS'S CIGARETTES

THE MARRIAGE OF PRINCESS MARY

WILLS'S CIGARETTES

THE KING AT THE CENOTAPH

WILLS'S CIGARETTES

THE PRINCE OF WALES AT OTTAWA

WILLS'S CIGARETTES

THE ROYAL CARRIAGE AT ASCOT

WILLS'S CIGARETTES

FUNERAL OF EARL HAIG.

WILLS'S CIGARETTES

RAILWAY CENTENARY EXHIBITION

WILLS'S CIGARETTES

REVIEW OF THE FLEET AT SPITHEAD

PLAYERS CIGARETTES

WILLS'S CIGARETTES

THE KING'S CONVALESCENCE

"A Masterpiece"

HUMBER "SNIPE"

HUMBER LIMITED, COVENTR

London Service Depot :
Canterbury Road, Kilburn, N.W.6

London Showrooms and Export Department :
Rootes Ltd., Devonshire House, Piccadilly, V

Overseas Representatives :

Australia and New Zealand—*Mr. C.E. Blayney, Rootes Ltd., Herald Buildings, Pitt Street, Sydney.*

India and Ceylon—*Mr. H. H. Lilley, P.O. Box 803, Bombay.*

South Africa—*Mr. H. C. Leon and Mr. John Good, Rootes Ltd., 40/40a, North British Buildings, C/r Commissioner and Simmonds Streets, Johannesburg.*

Burma, Malay and Far East—*Mr. A.F. Sanderson, P.O. Box 525, Singapore.*

Europe—*Mr. R. Escudier, Devonshire House, Piccadilly, London, W.1*

South America—*Mr.R.W.H.Cook, Florida 229, Office 1023-25, Buenos Aires.*

Meanwhile, Dillinger was beating his brains to find a way out of his predicament. He was confident that his friends would try to rescue him, but he realised that the jail in which he was being held presented too many difficulties for would-be rescuers. Perhaps Dillinger was not bright academically, but it cannot be denied that he had innate cunning. He decided to confess to the robbery at Bluffton knowing full well that it would mean his having to be transferred for questioning and identification on that charge. On 28 September he was indeed, sent to Allen County Jail at Lima and, as he had hoped, it was small, old and with few police on call. At about that time, the fugitives in Michigan City were beginning to find themselves in need of funds so, without much ado, they drove into a small Ohio town where they burst into the bank and made off with fifteen thousand dollars without a hitch. They now felt they were in a position to return Dillinger's favour. Using two cars, they drove to the jail in Lima, Ohio. There were Pierpont, Clark, Hamilton, Copeland, Makeley and Shouse. Pierpont, Clark and Makeley strode boldly into the jail and approached the desk at which Sheriff Jess Sarber was sitting. Also present were Sarber's wife, Lucy, and Deputy Wilbur Sharp. Pierpont said that he and his companions were officers from the Michigan State Penitentiary and that they had come to interrogate John Dillinger. The unsuspecting Sheriff asked the routine question, 'Let's see your credentials,' whereupon Harry Pierpont pulled out his pistol and snapped, 'Here's my credentials!'

Taken by surprise, the Sheriff made the mistake of reaching for his gun in a desk drawer. Harry Pierpont, nerves taut, fired twice. A fatal bullet struck the Sheriff in the side, pierced the abdomen, was deflected and severed the femoral artery in the thigh. In a convulsive reflex action, Sarber started to lurch to his feet and Makeley struck him across the head with a gun. Nevertheless the almost unconscious Sheriff staggered to his feet and Pierpont stepped in close and floored the luckless man with a vicious swipe of his pistol. Terrified, Mrs Sarber pleaded for her husband's life. She was ordered to get the keys from the cells and Dillinger was released. Gleefully he made off with his rescuers.

Sarber was rushed to hospital where he died, but not before he had identified Harry Copeland as one of the assailants. Later Mrs Sarber and Deputy Sharp identified Harry Pierpont from a mug-shot and named him as the killer of the Sheriff. Soon the rest of the gang were identified. Meanwhile the gang started to run amok. On 14 October 1933 they held up four policemen in their police station in Auburn, Indiana, and got away with a sub-machine gun, sawed off shotguns, pistols and rifles. They also took the badges from the hapless policemen for good measure.

On 14 October the Central National Bank at Green Castle, Indiana, was robbed of seventy-five thousand dollars in cash and bonds by Dillinger, Makeley and Copeland. Dillinger did his party piece, vaulting over the bank counter, a fact which was significant to the police when they heard about it.

However, a month later, Copeland was stupid, drunk or riled enough to pull a gun on a girl friend during an argument in the street. Police were called and before Harry could react, which lends credence to the idea that he was drunk, he was being carted off to jail. Edward Shouse took leave of his erstwhile comrades, stealing Russell Clark's new car to travel in. His friends were not unhappy about his sudden departure as it was the consensus of their opinion that the garrulous Shouse was a liability and a danger at all times.

On 23 November the American Bank and Trust Company at Racine, Wisconsin, had a visit from Dillinger, Makeley, Pierpont and Clark. Makeley stepped up to a teller's window and ordered assistant cashier Graham to put his hands up. The unfortunate man, who was hard of hearing, was poring over a column of figures and, without glancing up, told Makeley to go to another window, whereupon the irate bank-robber, lacking a sense of humour, fired at him, hitting him in the side and arm. As he fell, Graham's knee struck the alarm bell button and off went the alarm. Two officers came running in and Makeley fired again, felling one who was carrying a sub-machine gun, and Clark stopped the other one in his tracks. The gang made off with twenty-eight thousand dollars, the machine gun and four hostages whom they eventually released.

On 14 December the police, acting on information from an informer about the Michigan gang, were staked out at a Chicago garage when Red Hamilton arrived to pick up the gang's car. When challenged by one of the police officers, Sergeant Shanley, he pulled a gun, shot Shanley dead, and ran off.

The relentless Matt Leach took up the hunt for the Michigan gang and Shouse, who had artlessly come back from the West Coast, was caught in a police dragnet. In the shoot-out a policeman was accidentally killed by another policeman, but Shouse was captured unhurt. In another raid by a special police squad on an apartment block, the officers were greeted with a fierce fusillade which they returned in good measure, with machine guns and shot guns. When the shooting was over the police found three men shot to pieces, huddled in a corner of a room, and an armoury of weapons in the cupboards. Although the police had expected to catch the Michigan gang, they had in fact, with more luck than judgment, exterminated a trio of dangerous escaped convicts who were unconnected with Dillinger.

On 15 January 1934 in East Chicago, Indiana, a car braked to a halt outside the First National Bank just before closing time. Two men got out of the car. One of them, Dillinger, carried a trombone case. They strolled into the bank where Dillinger calmly opened the case and came up with a Thompson sub-machine gun. The other man, Hamilton, also produced a machine gun which he had been hiding under his coat. Dillinger ordered bank staff and clients to move to the back of the bank, but the bank manager who had happened to be talking on the phone, managed to gasp into the mouthpiece that the bank was being held up. He also managed to press a hidden button that activated an alarm at a police station not half a mile away.

A passing patrolman became suspicious and wandered into the bank to find himself confronting two deadly machine guns and he had no option but to join the other captives. Finally the bandits came running from the bank with a sackful of booty and two hapless hostages, the bank manager and the patrolman, only to find themselves up against another patrolman and three detectives who had just arrived on the scene. The patrolman, O'Malley, fired and hit Dillinger, but Dillinger, who was wearing a bulletproof vest, was merely jolted, and he opened up with his machine gun, mortally wounding the policeman.

As the bandits raced on to get to their car, Hamilton was hit by a bullet fired by one of the detectives. He was carrying the sack which contained the booty, twenty thousand round dollars, and Dillinger was loath to lose it. Firing short burst to beat back the detectives he went to Hamilton's rescue, yelling to him to hold on tight to the money. He managed to pack Hamilton and the sack into the car and it sped off down the street. Later Dillinger dropped off Hamilton at a doctor's, then went on his way. He was now wanted for murder.

The gang rendezvoused in Tucson and, as though they had not a care in the world, Makeley, Clark, Harry Pierpont and Dillinger, together with their girl friends, were soon hitting the high spots. However, by chance, Makeley and Clark had been involved in a fire at an hotel where they had been staying and one of the firemen had recognised them as members of the Michigan gang. Now the police were hot on the heels of the hoodlums. Makeley was arrested in a store and police and detectives went on to a house they already had under surveillance. They broke in and after a short struggle, Clark and his girl friend were dragged off to jail.

During all the excitement, Pierpont and his girl friend, approaching the house in a Buick, became suspicious and drove off in a hurry. But a nosy neighbour was sharp enough to spot the car number and notify the police. Pierpont was picked up after a brief struggle and he too was packed off to jail. Brimful of joy with their easy arrests, back went the police to stake out the house and sure enough Dillinger, together with his moll, turned up and, without a shot, the notorious bank robber found himself in the bag. The local police had something to crow about. They had hit the jackpot.

Dillinger was bitter about being transferred, with the connivance of the authorities, from Arizona where he would have faced lesser charges, to Indiana where he was wanted for murder. Spitting, spluttering and swearing, he had to be dragged aboard the aircraft especially chartered to take him back north. His language was foul as, like a mad dog, he

was chained to his seat and he never let up all the way to Chicago,
where he was transferred to Crown Point, Indiana.

There he found himself beset on all sides by reporters, photographers
and newsreel men fighting to get near him. Everyone wanted to get
into the act. The Prosecuting Attorney, Robert Estill, unthinkingly
consented to pose for a photograph with Dillinger, their arms casually
draped over each others shoulders in a friendly fashion. The picture,
when published, was to put the cat among the pigeons and the reper-
cussions were to continue for a long time.

Dillinger was incarcerated in Lake County Jail and he realised
immediately that nobody was going to be able to 'spring' him from the
solid brick walls and six armoured doors that barred the way to freedom. But once again, Dillinger was able to demonstrate his cunning
and audacity. With some ingenuity he fashioned a gun out of a piece
of wood, two razor blades and boot blacking, and used it to bluff his
way to grab a real pistol from Sheriff Blunk. Nobody was likely to
challenge a man such as Dillinger pointing anything that even re-
motely resembled a gun. Dillinger was joined by Herbert Youngblood,
a negro prisoner. They managed to pick up two sub-machine guns and
taking Blunk and Edgar Saager, a motor mechanic, with them, they
rode off in the Sheriff's car.

Dillinger dropped the hostages in the country and went on his way

Dillinger with the wooden
pistol he used to escape from
Crown Point Jail.

with Youngblood, having pulled off an astonishing coup that was reported in the press the whole world over. But by crossing the state line in a stolen car, Dillinger had violated a Federal law and now for the first time he had the F.B.I. on his tail. Youngblood was left to his own devices by Dillinger and he was killed in a shoot-out with the police on 16 March 1934.

Dillinger moved with his girl friend, Billie Frechette, to St Paul, Minnesota, and it did not take him long to assemble as vicious a gang of desperadoes as the U.S. had ever known. They were 'Red' Hamilton, 'Baby Face' Nelson, Homer Van Meter and Tommy Carroll. Dillinger also managed to get the brainy Eddie Green to work for him. It was left to Eddie to plot all the details involved in bank robberies.

On 6 March 1934, John Dillinger, Homer Van Meter, 'Baby Face' Nelson and Eddie Green called at the Security National Bank and Trust Company in Sioux City. Dillinger waved his sub-machine gun at the thirty-odd employees and customers and 'Baby Face' snarled at them not to dare move. He climbed on to a marble-topped table the better to cover the crowd and glanced casually through the window into the street where Tommy Carroll was standing by their car. Across the street, 'Red' Hamilton was trying to hold back a crowd of gawping people. Both hoodlums were armed with sub-machine guns. Nelson suddenly spotted a motorcycle policeman approaching and, not stopping to think, fired a burst right through the window, splintering it into fragments and sending the policeman spinning and sprawling on to the sidewalk, scattering the crowd in every direction.

The alarm had been raised and police officers were waiting to go into action as Dillinger and his men emerged from the bank, herding along ten hostages. The police were powerless as the gangsters drove off with five of the hostages, four of them women, and fifty thousand dollars. After a running battle with police pursuers and after dumping their hostages, the gangsters arrived safely back in Minneapolis.

Six days later, Dillinger, Nelson, Green, Van Meter, Carroll, Hamilton and a new member of the gang, John Paul Chase, drove to the rear of the First National Bank of Mason City, Iowa. Leaving Chase at the wheel of the car and Nelson standing guard alongside it, the others went into the bank. They did not realise that high in the lobby, perched in a bullet-proof cage, bank guard Tom Walter, armed with tear gas, watched their every movement and was ready to blast away at the drop of a hat.

Then Carroll caught sight of him and coolly raised his sub-machine gun to keep Walter's head down with well-aimed bursts of bullets. Walter did, however, manage to lob out an occasional tear gas bomb, but only with the effect of adding to the general confusion. Outside, Nelson was having his own troubles with the usual crowd of stupid 'rubbernecks', and irked, he fired a few bursts in their direction, but failed to daunt the crowd. One man, seemingly quite oblivious to what

102

was going on, casually approached the astonished Nelson and had his legs shot from under him for his temerity.

Suddenly the alarm bell began to clang and as the bandits came hurtling pell-mell from the bank bearing their sacks of booty and hustling a group of hostages, both Dillinger and Hamilton were shot in the shoulder. They did not even slow down and driving their terrified hostages before them they piled into the car, and forced the hostages to line the running boards. The getaway car went careering away followed by the police. After a while the bank raiders succeeded in shaking off the police and they then dropped off the hostages. The gangsters finally got back to St Paul where a doctor was forced to attend to the wounds of Dillinger and Hamilton.

Dillinger went to ground with Billie Frechette, but before long the caretaker of the house where they were staying became suspicious of their comings and goings and voiced his suspicions to the police. The F.B.I. were notified. Lawmen arrived at the house and right away Agent Coulter encountered Van Meter in a corridor. Quick on the uptake, Van Meter opened fire and bolted, managing to escape. Dillinger, with Billie trailing behind him, came charging out with machine gun blazing. They made their way down the back staircase to the garage where Billie backed out a car and picked up Dillinger just as he was struck in the leg by a bullet. They drove off to the safety of Eddie Green's place in Minneapolis where Eddie, forewarned by Homer Van Meter, was waiting for them and he lost no time in getting a doctor to attend to Dillinger.

In the apartment Dillinger had so hastily vacated the police found Eddie Green's address, but by the time they got there the birds had flown and all that remained were a lot of Eddie's clothes, personal effects and a few rounds of ammunition. The F.B.I. decided to stake out the apartment and were on hand when two negro sisters arrived, having been sent to pick up the belongings of a man they knew as T. J. Randall. The F.B.I. agents then moved to keep watch from inside the house of the two women.

The agents' move was rewarded when a car pulled up across the street and a man got out and started walking toward the house where they were watching and waiting. The F.B.I. decided to shoot first and save questions until later. Eddie Green, a married man, fell mortally wounded. However, it was eight days before he died during which time he told the agents everything he knew about his criminal associates including Harry Sawyer, the big-time racketeer who ran the town.

Dillinger and Billie had gone to Mooresville, Dillinger's hometown, for a family visit before going to Chicago. The F.B.I. were hard on the heels of the gangster and on 9 April 1934 in Chicago, they nearly caught up with him. Dillinger had driven to meet a friend at a saloon. He dropped Billie off to go on into the saloon, while he parked the car. She walked straight into the arms of waiting F.B.I. agents and was immediately arrested. Meanwhile, having parked the car at the end of the block, Dillinger was walking towards the saloon when he realised that something was wrong. He rushed back to his car and drove off. Later he told his attorney, Piquette, to find out what had happened to Billie and that if she was in trouble with the police Piquette was to represent her.

Three days after his narrow escape, Dillinger and Van Meter held up a police officer and forced him to open the armoury in City Hall where they replenished their own armoury. Dillinger was preparing for action as all over the country the press were exaggerating rumours of his latest activities and making wild speculations about his possible whereabouts. Meanwhile Dillinger and his gang planned to rendezvous at a popular summer resort near Mercer, Wisconsin. The Little Bohemia, the roadhouse where they had chosen to stay out of season, was deep in the woods on the edge of Star Lake. It seemed a perfect spot for a hardworking, hardpressed gang of hoodlums and their molls to recuperate and plot their future moves in safety.

On 20 April 1934 Homer Van Meter and two girls arrived to look over the place. In the evening Dillinger, Hamilton, Carroll, 'Baby Face' Nelson and his wife and two other girls arrived in two cars to join them. Their baggage included machine guns, rifles and plenty of ammunition and when one of the porters unsuspectingly remarked about the weight Nelson sneered, 'Mind you don't rupture yourself.'

It is not surprising that the proprietor of the lodge, Mr Wanatka and his wife, soon became suspicious of their guests and Mrs Wanatka managed to inform Henry Voss, who owned a lodge a few miles away, that she feared that she was harbouring the notorious Dillinger gang. Voss telephoned the F.B.I. and was told to be waiting at Rhinelander, the nearest airfield to Mercer, fifty miles away. F.B.I. agents arrived on 22 April and commandeered cars to drive to the Little Bohemia.

While the agents were moving in to surround the lodge, the proprietors' collie dogs, Spot and Prince, started barking. There then followed a burst of gunfire. Three local men who happened to be

Mrs Wanatka with her dogs, and *below right* the Little Bohemia roadhouse.

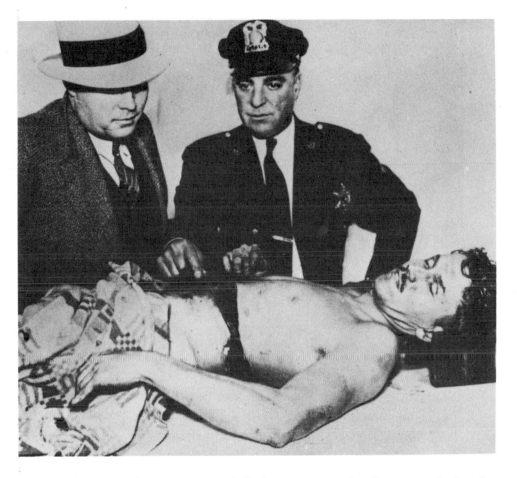

Above, Federal agent
W. Carter Baum, killed by
the Dillinger gang. *Right,* the
end of Baby Face Nelson.
Below, the top window of the
Little Bohemia through which
the gang escaped.

driving by were hit; one was killed, two were badly wounded. The Dillinger gang, fully alerted, escaped by a rear window leaving their womenfolk hiding in the basement. Dillinger, Van Meter, Carroll and Hamilton made off to the right along the lakeside. Nelson, who had delayed to shoot at his pursuers (killing Special Agent W. Carter Baum), lost sight of his companions and moved off to the right. All the gangsters managed to get clean away. But the next day Van Meter was driving a stolen car with Dillinger sitting beside him and 'Red' Hamilton dozing in the back, when a police car started to overtake them and the police opened fire. Homer Van Meter, who was a brilliant driver, shook off pursuit but not before 'Red' Hamilton had been fatally wounded.

Realising that his face was too easily recognisable for his own safety, Dillinger decided in May to undergo some plastic surgery. He was lucky to survive the crude operations which did little to alter his appearance. In any case his obsidian eyes, in those days before contact lenses, were unalterable and unmistakable.

On 7 June 1934 Tommy Carroll foolishly reached for his gun when he walked into a police trap and was immediately cut down by five bullets. Dillinger seemed quite unperturbed when he heard news of the fate of his comrade in arms. He had his own fish to fry and it was time again for frying.

The arsenal Dillinger left
behind at the roadhouse.

On 30 June, the same day that Hitler prepared for the 'Night of the
Long Knives', John Dillinger and Homer Van Meter, machine guns at
the ready, strode menacingly into the Merchants' National Bank at
South Bend, Indiana, where Dillinger introduced himself by firing a
burst through the ceiling. Outside, Chase was waiting at the wheel of
their car and Nelson was watching with his machine gun cocked. A
patrolman on traffic duty, hearing the sound of Dillinger's gratuitous
machine gun bursts, unwisely as it happened, approached the bank to
investigate and was promptly shot dead by Nelson. Once more the
gang took hostages and mounted them on the running boards of the
getaway car. Police arriving on the scene cut loose with their weapons
and scored hits on a bank cashier and another official, while the
robbers got away with twenty-eight thousand dollars.

On 21 July 1934 Melvin Purvis, the F.B.I. agent who had been in
charge of the Bohemian Lodge fiasco, received a hot tip from police in
East Chicago, Indiana, about the whereabouts of John Dillinger. The
police were in contact with an informer, Anna Sage, manageress of a
whorehouse, who was prepared to set Dillinger up. Purvis made the
necessary arrangements and the special Dillinger squad was alerted. It
had been learned that Dillinger planned to visit the cinema with
friends who included Anna Sage, but as it was not known for sure
which of two cinemas he would be patronising, it was decided to stake
out both. When it was reported to Purvis that Dillinger had arrived at

the Biograph cinema, Purvis had the agents covering the other cinema race, post haste, to the Biograph.

Dillinger had been clearly seen; there was no mistake about his identity. He went into the cinema with his two companions and the F.B.I. agents decided to nail him after the show which, intending it to be his last, they hoped he would enjoy. So for just over two hours the F.B.I. agents and police waited fretfully in strategic positions around the theatre while, blissfully unaware of the preparations outside, Dillinger and his companions, the treacherous Anna Sage and Polly Hamilton, watched the movie, *Manhattan Melodrama*.

Just after 10.30 p.m. the people began drifting out of the theatre and tense lawmen saw Dillinger come ambling out, chatting with his two women. Anna Sage, Dillinger's Rahab, dropped back. Polly, suddenly spotting a man with a gun, yelled a warning to Dillinger as she made a dive for cover. Dillinger started to run but it was too late. He managed to reach an alley when he staggered and fell with four bullets in him. One knocked an eye out. He had not been given a chance. It had been a successful seek-and-destroy operation.

Of course there were those people who thought that the manner in which Dillinger had been shot down was deplorable; there were those who even thought he had been some sort of a Robin Hood, and of course, there were those who said that Dillinger was an unfortunate victim of society. As he lay like a dead dog in the gutter there were the frenzied ghouls who fought to dip their handkerchiefs in his blood for souvenirs and later, those who had to be prevented from robbing his grave. Were they too victims of society? Are such people really the victims of society or is society the victim of such people?

Dillinger was just what he seemed to be – a shiftless thief without thought, a killer without conscience, whom the press had found good copy. Now they would have to hurry to keep the kettle boiling by providing a successor. So 'Baby Face' Nelson was immediately promoted to Public Enemy Number One.

An innocent victim of the gangs, New York, 1934.

Fashion on parade

I CAN REMEMBER MY FATHER WEARING SPATS OVER HIS shoes. They were like short gaiters, made of a soft grey or beige material with buttons down the side, which turned shoes into boots and were considered to be very 'posh' by one and all. My father also wore silk ties which cost anything from 4s. 6d. to 7s. 6d. each, well-cut made-to-measure suits and light overcoats with raglan sleeves. He wore trilby hats – never bowlers – and sometimes he wore a sort of fedora with a turndown brim which he called a 'jibber-jabber'. Usually for work, he wore a cloth cap, badge of the working class. He never wore sports jackets or flannels.

Menswear shops sold good shirts for five shillings and tip-top Van Heusen shirts for 10s. 6d. At the Man's Shop, Harrods, shirts made to measure cost 21s. For that sort of money, every shirt and collar was laundered before despatch; a pattern was cut for every customer and kept for future reference: all shirts were made in Harrods' own workrooms and all buttonholes were handmade. The material used was the finest woven poplin obtainable. Harrods also sold handmade English foulard silk ties, lined with crepe silk and crepe silk handkerchiefs to match at 12s. 6d. a set.

By the mid-thirties, youths were beginning to be more fashion-conscious than they had been during the late twenties and early thirties. Shirts, purported to be as worn by famous film stars, were all the fashion. I had a George Raft shirt, a Dick Powell shirt and a George Brent shirt – but not all at the same time. I wore a very snazzy mid-blue Clark Gable sports jacket with a Max Baer back and patch pockets. Max Baer was a popular world champion heavyweight boxer about that time. The back of the jacket was gathered and pouched from a yoke to a fixed half-belt at the back. The jacket lasted me through a pair of grey worsted flannels and a pair of grey gabardines, and I went off into the army wearing it. It finally went back home to hang in the wardrobe until I came out of the army more than six years later. I last saw it on the back of our odd-job man sometime in 1957. I was very fond of that jacket.

The overcoat, too, that saw me into the army, was heavy, belted and

A tailored suit from Burberry, 1933.

had a big storm collar. It was of the finest Crombie material, navy with
a hint of a fine silver fleck. I was proud of that coat and for the first
month in the Forces, until we had some sort of a kit issue, I was glad to
use it as a blanket. I sent it back home eventually and wore it once or
twice while on furlough. When I was demobbed, I took it back into
service for a while. It was a good coat and weighed a ton. They do not
make coats like that any more. Shoulders nowadays are not built to
support such weights.

For a long time in the thirties, women's styles seemed to be based on
tubular, elongated shapes with wide raised shoulders, but gradually

A 7 guinea coat and dress from Swan and Edgar, 1938.

skirts became shorter, fuller and pleated. Women wore suits, fur collars and hats. Slacks were worn on holidays and for weekends in the country. A curious contraption known as a suspender belt was worn to support the stockings. Men considered it very titillating to catch a glimpse of a girl hoisting her skirt a few inches to fasten a stocking.

Whereas the influence of Paris was predominent in the fashions of the well-heeled, mass produced dresses in American materials and styles were worn by the average girl with an eye on Hollywood, prior to World War Two. There were shops which claimed that the shoes they sold had actually been worn by Hollywood stars just once or twice for the purpose of filming. These shops, mostly in Soho, did brisk business.

When I was drawing fashion sketches just before the war, I used to seek inspiration in fashion books from Paris, Brussels, Vienna and New York. There were masses of them. I found it easier to design coats, ('mantles' to the trade) rather than dresses, and I would pick up many ideas from watching the windows of dress shops and by keeping my eyes open on visits to fashion houses.

The girl I married wore excellent clothes. Her father, a cutter-designer of model mantles and suits, made his samples for her size. These garments, exquisitely cut and hand stitched, were of the best materials. In those days, suits for women meant jackets and skirts and were extremely popular.

As the decade ended with war becoming the way of life for millions, fashions changed drastically. By December 1939 many young men had exchanged their 'civvies' for uniforms and battledress was drab and far from elegant. Women's clothes had, of necessity, become more practical and austere and women in slacks were to be seen everywhere. The shape of women's large posteriors, something everyone is used to by now, was a revelation in those far off days. Soon, many girls were also entering the services and I thought they looked particularly unattractive in uniform. Perhaps, at that time, I had a jaundiced eye.

The fire-raisers

NOT LONG AFTER LEAVING PUBLIC SCHOOL, MY COUSIN went on a motoring holiday to Germany. He drove a spanking new, shiny red M.G. Midget sports coupé, very popular with well-heeled youths of the mid-thirties. I spent a day with him on his return from Germany and he told me what a 'spiffing' time he had had and that, in his opinion, the Nazis were not at all as black as much of the world press painted them. He sported a swastika pennant on his car and a German sticker or two on the windscreen. I told him to get rid of them, fast.

'Oh!' he said. 'They're just souvenirs. What are you – some sort of a Bolshie or something?'

When he asked me to drive with him to pick up some rolls of film he had left at the chemist's to be developed, I told him I had no intention of riding in a car flying a swastika, and I got a supercilious grin for my trouble. I said I would wait for him to get back. When he returned, he was livid. He said vandals had not only removed his swastika pennant but had made deep, ragged scratches with a knife or nail in the paint-work on both sides of his car. I told him that my heart bled for him and that he was lucky that the vandals had not also smashed his wind-screen because of the German stickers.

My cousin always wore his O.T.C. (Officers' Training Corps) badge in his lapel. Just before the war broke out he went to America and has been there ever since. I wonder if he still wears his badge? He was one of those peculiar people who loved badges.

By the mid-thirties Mussolini and Hitler, despite their ranting and raving and downright aggresive policies, were attracting considerable admiration from many people all over the world. Would be Führers were bobbing up out of cesspools all over the place to organise Fascist parties and were aping their dictator heroes in every conceivable manner. They too had to have their symbols and trappings. They found variations on the Nazi swastika; they had the flags, the banners, the military style uniforms, belts with big buckles and shiny black jackboots. They also had the Nazi style parades and tried to organise spectacular gatherings.

In Britain, Oswald Mosley, one time up-and-coming Labour M.P., hurriedly decided to jump on the band wagon. He became leader of the British Fascists and adopted a flash of lightning in a circle (which became known as 'the flash in the pan') as his 'swastika' symbol. He and his officers wore black, military style uniforms, shiny peaked caps, shiny black belts and shiny jackboots. His minions had to be content with an issue of black shirt or sweater, black trousers and a black belt with a big silver buckle, a formidable weapon when wound round wrist and fist and used as a knuckleduster. These Fascists, for the most part a nondescript looking bunch in ordinary clothes, appeared more impressive as a cohesive force in their black funwear. A Fascist in uniform considered himself a fully fledged stormtrooper after the German fashion and was ready to ape the part at all times.

When Fascist speakers held street meetings they had no patience to answer what they considered to be awkward questions, and their black-shirted bravos and layabouts were always there in force around the speaker's platform, eager to pitch in against hecklers and questioners and whoever else happened to be in the way and looked easy game. However there were anti-Fascists, including Socialists and Communists, who were reluctant to allow these surrogate Nazis to preach their poison without hindrance.

I was involved in many fights at Fascist and anti-Fascist meetings and rallies, including the great Fascist Cable Street fiasco where there was a good deal of passion and naked violence; but there were youngsters who liked to fight for the sake of fighting and politics did not always come into it. Irresponsible youths picked sides like they do for the Oxford–Cambridge boat race. However the whole concept of Fascist and anti-Fascist warfare in the streets of Britain was both repugnant and frightening to many of the public who realised all too well, from the examples of Germany, Austria and Romania, the dangers that confronted them. Many who had admired Mussolini did not admire the menacing Hitler. The Germans, the enemy of World War One, were still not generally liked. Hitler's bombast was familiar to radio listeners; his spectacular demolition of the Treaty of Versailles and his growing military power as fearsomely demonstrated in the so-called civil war in Spain, made the apparent inevitability of another world war a dominant factor in the lives of the British people for several years before the war finally erupted and resolved the general British attitude to Fascism.

Until then, the Government seemed powerless as Europe moved inexorably toward the holocaust. To fight Fascists in the streets seemed to be all that one could do at the time.

The Nazi rise to prominence in German elections in the period of the mid-twenties and early thirties was countered by improvement in

Mosley inspects his female
fascists, July 1933.

the position of left wing parties at the polls. But the Nazis, with their
masterly propaganda and callous brutality in the streets, with their
continual provoking of ministerial crises that meant constant elections
and disruption, were able to whittle away the rickety props holding up
the already shaky Weimar Republic. The Nazis deftly used democracy
to make a mockery of every manifestation of it, to confuse the left wing
parties and the milk and water moderates who bickered among themselves and failed to unite to combat the hydra-headed monster rearing
before them.

Papen, the great survivor,
1938.

The decrepit President Hindenburg favoured representatives of the
Reichswehr and monopolistic German industry. He dismissed the left
wing Bruening as Chancellor and appointed the crafty survivor, Von
Papen, in his place. Von Papen swept out top Republican officials,
replacing them with Nationalists, thus opening the way for the Nazis.
In the July elections of 1932 they captured two hundred and thirty
seats in the Reichstag. But in the November elections they had a
serious setback, losing two million votes and thirty-four seats. Von

The new religion. Berlin
University students combine
the sign of the cross with the
sign of the swastika while *far
right* postmen in Berlin
spread the gospel.

113

Papen was forced to resign and was replaced by Von Schleicher who, in his turn, was compelled to relinquish his office.

On 30 January, doddering Hindenburg appointed Adolf Hitler as Chancellor. Hitler, in the saddle, was ready to ride rough shod over all opposition. The police forces were infiltrated by Nazis and purged of Republicans. Nazis brawled with opponents all over the country. Hindenburg dissolved the Reichstag and Hitler proclaimed that if the following elections did not give him a majority he would rule outside the constitution. Goering's remodelled police forces and S.A. gangs went into action immediately, raiding Communist headquarters and faking evidence against opponents of the Nazis. The S.A. went on a rampage of murder, torture and intimidation against Republicans, Catholics, Communists, Jews and anybody else who got in the way.

Yet, despite this vicious and sustained campaign, opposition to the Nazis continued and when the Communist groups finally succeeded in uniting under a single leadership and appealed to the masses to join with them against the Fascist dictatorship, the Nazis became alarmed. They realised that somehow they must crush the Communist party in one fell coup to prevent the backlash against them and it had to be done with the appearance of legality. Something must be done to utterly discredit the Communist Party. What was needed was a super plot even more hair-raising than the false Zinoviev letter which had been successfully used in Britain to discredit the Labour Party in the previous decade. This was no problem for the ruthless, highly organised Nazi Party machine and Goering's Nazi-corrupted police forces.

On 22 February 1933 Goering prepared for the big show by enrolling S.A. and Stahlhelm as auxiliary police and issuing them with swastika armbands. On 27 February, just after nine in the morning, the Reichstag building was seen to be alight and it was discovered that incendiary devices had been placed throughout the building. The fire service did little to prevent the fire from spreading and the building was soon well ablaze. Flames leapt into the members' chamber and brought the vast gilded dome crashing into the inferno. A bemused man had been apprehended on the premises and taken to police headquarters. He was a Dutchman named Van der Lubbe and was dubbed a Communist. The Nazis had their Zinoviev letter and were ready to act in no uncertain manner.

Goering's task forces set to work at once to implement repressive measures against their enemies. Communists, Democrats and anybody else who dared to oppose or criticise the Nazis, were rounded up. By 1 March the Communists had been castrated, the Democrats had been demolished and the powerful groups of German trade unionists were in a state of shock. On 5 March came the General Election and the Nazis won 288 out of 647 seats in the Reichstag and promptly arrested all the Communist members and the one Socialist member. They struck out ruthlessly in all directions, giving their opponents no chance to recover.

The Reichstag building at the height of the blaze.

Communist and Socialist publications were banned and a state of emergency was declared.

The new venue of the Reichstag was the garrison church at Potsdam. No Communist members were present. They were either in prison or in exile. The Reichstag passed an Enabling Bill giving Hitler powers of dictatorship for four years. It was passed by 441 with 91 against – all those against being Social Democrats whose spokesman, Wels, made a courageous speech against the Act. Amongst those who did vote for the Act, however, were former Reichschancellor Bruening, Dr Ludwig Kass of the Centre Party, and Theodor Heuss, later to be the first President of the German Federal Republic – the man who was subsequently welcomed to Britain in 1958 with a speech by Queen Elizabeth which disregarded the darker aspects of Anglo-German relations in the past. Having passed the Enabling Act the Reichstag then dissolved itself. Weimar disappeared and democracy and the Republican flag disappeared with it. The Nazi swastika symbolised the new Germany.

As well as Van der Lubbe, the Germans had arrested others as being implicated in the firing of the Reichstag and they staged a show trial at Leipzig beginning in September. On trial were Van der Lubbe, the German Communist leader, Torgler, and three Bulgarians – writer Georgi Dimitroff, student Blagoi Popoff and shoemaker Wassil Taneff. Only Van der Lubbe was actually accused of arson and to any impartial witness he was so obviously an idiot that it seemed incredible that

Van der Lubbe, accused of firing the Reichstag.

the Nazis should slip up so badly in not having selected a more plausible candidate to be scapegoat. Van der Lubbe sat with downcast eyes, gaping mouth drooling, and seemed to take no interest in the trial. On one occasion when he laughed suddenly and was asked by the judge what he was laughing at, he replied that he found the proceedings funny. Often inaudible in his replies to questions, the Dutchman was a pathetic figure. Dimitroff, however, was a man to be reckoned with. He was cool, confident and clever. He repeatedly riled the blustering Goering who was giving evidence at the trial, provoking him with shrewdly barbed questions to rave and splutter and yell almost incoherent threats above the pandemonium in court. Goering's performance and antics marked him as no less an idiot, but infinitely more dangerous, than the unfortunate Van der Lubbe. But it was Dimitroff, urging his fervent belief in political revolution but denying any connection with the firing of the Reichstag, who dominated the trial.

The Allies of World War One with their own axes to grind did nothing to counter the German menace with any sort of common front or joint action. In fact, many politicians in the ranks of the former Allies and from other countries professed to see merit and example in Nazism, and some opportunists were quick to ape the new brand of Fascism. Nor did the Church drag its feet behind Hitler's bold advance.

In 1960 when it was no longer considered fashionable to be openly anti-Semitic, Bishop Otto Dibelius admitted that he had been anti-Semitic but claimed that he had changed his spots. It is on record that in April 1933, when he had been Lutheran General Superintendent, he made a shortwave broadcast in which he appealed to the Americans to show understanding for the Nazi boycott of Jewish shops. In 1933 German Catholic bishops published a pastoral letter, rejoicing in the strangling of the popular spirit and two weeks later, when the Catholic Centre Party was spontaneously dissolved and a message of congratulations sent to Hitler, the Pope concluded a concordat with the Nazi Government, thus presenting Hitler with a political and moral victory as well as an air of respectability.

Before long, international notables were making the pilgrimage to Germany to visit the new Messiah. Arnold Toynbee, the historian who in World War One had spotlighted German atrocities, visited the new Germany and came back convinced of Hitler's peaceful intentions. Poseur and politician, Lloyd George, man of the hour in World War One, took his farewell from a visit to Hitler at Berchtesgaden with a Nazi salute which he said had been a joke. If so, it was a sick one. In describing Hitler as the George Washington of Germany – an insult to Washington – he said Hitler was the greatest German of the century.

Others who went to pay homage to Hitler were worshippers with ambitions to emulate him in their own countries. These included Oswald Mosley, the Blackshirt leader from Britain; the pederast

The Reichstag fire trial.
Above, Torgler declares his
innocence. *Top right,* Van der
Lubbe sits downcast.

Right, Goering arrives to give
evidence at the trial.
Far right, martial law arrives
in Germany, 1932.

Degrelle, the Belgian Fascist; Seyss Inquart, the Austrian traitor, and Vidkun Quisling, the odious Norwegian whose name has become universally synonymous with the word 'traitor'.

In 1938 after the Anschluss, the Cardinal Archbishop of Vienna, Theodor Innitzer, in a letter to Gauleiter Buerckel, added in his own hand, 'Heil Hitler'. The Austrian bishops expressed their approval of the incorporation of Austria and Germany and praised the Nazi movement.

In general, most foreign businessmen and tourists visiting Germany after Hitler had come to power saw only what was on the surface and were quite content not to scratch too deeply.

119

Night of the long knives

A SOLDIER I MET IN INDIA DURING THE WAR, WITH WHOM I went exploring Old Delhi on several occasions, told me his father had been a British officer and his mother a German nurse. His parents had met in Cologne where his father was garrisoned after World War One. My acquaintance also told me that he had been born in Germany and after a few years his family had come to England until his father's demobilisation. They had returned to Germany soon after, when his father had taken an appointment with a British company importing German wines and had gone to live in Cologne.

My acquaintance said he had attended a British school as it was his father's wish. Most of his relations were German as his father, an orphan, had few, but he and his parents had spent most of their holidays in England as well as going there on frequent business trips. He told me about his German relations, two of them uncles who were in the S.S. He said they strutted around in uniform and that they always seemed to be at loggerheads with his father who was, more often than not, downright rude and insulting to them. But my acquaintance assured me that their skins were thicker than a pumpkin's.

He told me that he had been driving to Munich with his mother and father not long after Hitler had come to power and as they were approaching the suburbs they saw a huge warning sign which read, 'Dangerous Curve! Slow down! Jews excepted!' He said that his father had taken a dim view of that, not because he had any particular liking for Jews, but because he thought dislikes should be personal, not instruments of policy. 'However,' said my acquaintance, 'my father certainly had no love for Germans.' I remember him grinning enigmatically as he added, 'I think that is why he married my mother.'

I made no comment but asked him what he himself thought of the Nazis. He just gave me a twist on an old saying. He said, 'All Nazis are bastards, but thank God all bastards are not Nazis.'

Some months before Hitler went to Venice to consult with Mussolini,

120

Portrait of a Jew-hater –
Julius Streicher.

Below, Captain Rœhm,
leader of the Brownshirts.

the Austrian Chancellor Dollfuss had spent a few days at Riccione with
the Italian dictator and told him, among other things, about Hitler
and the sexual perversions and predilections of his henchmen that even
shocked the not-so-easily shocked Mussolini. Hitler came to Venice on
14 June 1934, accompanied by his entourage, and the conduct of
Brueckner, Hitler's adjutant – a bisexual pervert – and the conduct of
other Germans in the party, caused protests from Mussolini. He
warned Hitler that the activities of some leading Nazis were already
common gossip and were causing considerable uneasiness among Nazi
supporters in Italy. He specifically mentioned Roehm, commander of
the S.A., Edmond Heines, storm troop group leader at Breslau, Karl
Ernst and Julius Streicher, editor of the notorious anti-Semitic and
pornographic *Der Stürmer* and former school teacher, dismissed by the
Nuremburg school authorities because of charges of pederasty. Mussolini suggested it would be wise if Hitler got rid of them. Hitler was
enraged, but he had more than an inkling that President Hindenburg
too, was pressing for much the same thing. The German army, uneasy
about the growing power of Roehm and his massive private army of
Brownshirts, wanted him destroyed

More important to Hitler was the fact that Krupp and other leading
German industrialists who had backed him to the hilt were now
threatening to withdraw their support for the Nazi regime. Hitler was
considering how best to meet this threat from the right.

On 21 June he went to the Neudeck home of Hindenburg but was refused entry. He was told by Goering and Blomberg that the President had said that unless the heads of the S.A. were dismissed, martial law would be declared and Goering would take over as Chief of Police and Blomberg would take control of the military. Hitler insisted on seeing the President and, when he finally got his way, Hindenburg repeated his threat. Hitler resolved to call a meeting of the S.A. He was fully aware of the threat posed by Roehm but hesitated before taking action. After all, Roehm controlled three million Brownshirts.

On 29 June the *Völkische Beobachter* had published an article by General Von Blomberg purporting to be a reply to foreign news services which had reported a plot against Hitler, and while assuring Hitler of the army's loyalty to the new regime, warned that the army, not the S.A., had the true right to be representative of the power of a unified Germany. On that same morning Himmler had flown from Berlin to Godesberg and presented Hitler with a dossier of faked details of an S.A. plot which was due to be put into operation the very next day. Government buildings were to be occupied and a death squad had been detailed to kill Hitler. The S.A. would take to the streets armed with weapons supplied by General Von Leeb from stores in old army depots.

Hitler had been ordered to report to Krupp's headquarters where he found himself confronted by the heads of this vast complex industrial organisation, other powerful industrialists and Goering acting as the 'honest broker'. They presented an ultimatum. It was unequivocal. Unless Hitler got rid of Roehm and a number of other specified Nazi leaders they would withdraw their support for the Nazi regime. Coming from Krupp this was particularly hard for Hitler to take. The last original member of the Krupp family, whose son-in-law had only assumed the name on his marriage to the daughter Bertha, had committed suicide after a newspaper exposé of a sordid scandal involving homosexual relations and perverted practices with waiters in Italian hotels.

It was generally believed by the industrial and Nazi hierarchy that it was through homosexual connections that Hitler had met Krupp in the first place. It was even said that Dollfuss, the Austrian dictator, had been murdered by the Nazis because he had in his possession an authentic affadavit declaring that Hitler had been a male prostitute in Vienna and later in Munich which enabled him to move in corrupt bourgeois political circles and enlist the backing of Krupp.

But Hitler had already made his decision and was prepared to use the situation to his advantage. He would make his future position unassailable. He had no compunction about double-crossing Roehm, although it was Roehm who had given him his first job in Munich, that of political spy for the army. Of course, Hitler had been quite aware of the activities of Roehm and Ernst. The Gestapo had had them

Roehm and his cronies at the
Nuremberg party rally, 1933.

Austrian Chancellor Dollfuss
at a rally of the 'Patriotic
Front', 1933.

Nazi leaders Frick and Strasser, 1932.

under surveillance for a long time and Goering had repeatedly drawn Hitler's attention to the danger that Roehm's power presented to them.

Hitler hesitated no longer. Not only would he wipe out Roehm and his retinue of catamites, but striking out ruthlessly in all directions, he would rid himself of everybody that he considered would, or could, be of danger to his absolute power. He ordered Goering and Himmler to Berlin to take command of the situation there and flew to Munich with Goebbels and a carefully selected party of hatchetmen to deal personally with those men he had marked for death. Hitler's plane landed at Oberwiesenfeld, near Munich, at four o'clock on the morning of 30

124

Supermen with plenty of weight to throw about; Goering meets a gauleiter at a Nazi rally.

June. His general plan had already been set in motion and when he reached the Brown House it was already occupied by the Reichswehr.

Adolf Wagner, Bavarian Minister of the Interior, had been alerted to deal with Major Schneidhuber, Police President, and Schmidt, Munich S.A. leader. Wagner, an unstable dipsomaniac with a bullet embedded in his brain since World War One, had acted swiftly, summoning to a drinking party at the Ministry a number of people including Schneidhuber (whose wife belonged to a prominent Bavarian Jewish family of industrialists) Schmidt and others marked by Hitler for slaughter.

The guests were arranged around a large table in such a way that each intended victim was seated alongside the man assigned to kill him. When Hitler arrived at Oberwiesenfeld, a telephone message to Wagner from the airfield was the signal for the bloodbath. What transpired was reminiscent of what took place at a Chicago party almost a decade before, when gangster Al Capone, armed with a baseball bat, had battered to death his old friends, Giunta, Scalise and Anselmi. (See the previous book in this series, *Spotlight on the Twenties*.)

In 1942 *Die Zeitung*, a German language newspaper published in Britain stated, 'Wagner's guests were slaughtered with the heavy stone beer mugs that are used in Munich. The skull of Police President Schneidhuber was split open by one blow.' These murders have also been attributed to Sep Dietrich and his S.S. murder squad.

Hitler congratulated the killers, Wagner, Esser, Weber and Buch, all well known sexual deviants, before setting out for Bad Wiessee where Roehm was staying. Accompanying Hitler on the forty-mile journey was his bodyguard which included Brueckner, Maurice, Dietrich and Schaub. The motorcade was headed by an army armoured car.

It was seven in the morning when the convoy arrived outside the small Hotel Hanslbauer where Roehm had established himself and his henchmen. There was no visible sign of the alleged impending S.A. revolt. A single S.A. guard at the door of the inn offered no resistance to the early visitors and nobody else seemed to be abroad. White with passion, oblivious to the obvious absence of any military activity or preparations for a coup d'état, Hitler stormed into the building and came face to face with Roehm's aide-de-camp who had been awakened by the commotion. Hitler struck him violently across the face with a hippopotamus hide whip, thrust past him and burst into Roehm's room, taking the sinister pervert by surprise.

Roehm and many of his men were arrested and clapped into hand-cuffs. In one room Obergruppenfuehrer Heines was found sharing his bed with Schmidt, his young chauffeur, and when startled awake he began to protest and resist. Brueckner and Maurice, both sexual perverts themselves, shot Heine and his *Lustknabe* dead. An hour later the convoy was on its way back to Munich. On the road a column of trucks carrying armed S.A. men on the way to Wiessee was encountered. Hitler had them disarmed and ordered their officers to take them home. Roehm and his men were removed to Munich and imprisoned. The S.S. and Gestapo continued rounding up persons listed by the Gestapo and these included some S.A. leaders. Most, however, were political opponents and others who had fallen foul of the head hunters. By about two in the afternoon more than two hundred people had been arrested and sent to Stadelheim prison.

The executions began soon after, with firing squads having to be relieved from their onerous task every so often. Hitler himself had selected the names of those to be executed from the list prepared by the

Hitler and Goering ten years after their abortive putsch.

Goering police.

Gestapo, but as a gesture he wished to spare his old comrade Roehm the ignominy of death by firing squad. He ordered that a revolver loaded with a single cartridge be placed in Roehm's cell. The inference was obvious but, crouched in a corner, sweating with terror, Roehm ignored the invitation to do away with himself and after a while a warder entered the cell and, without comment, removed the pistol.

A few seconds later, Roehm jumped to his feet as two S.S. men armed with revolvers entered the cell. One was Eicke, who studied Roehm coldly, then levelling his pistol with calm deliberation pumped several bullets into the fat body of the erstwhile leader of three million Brownshirts. Bending over his prostrate victim, Eicke fired a shot into the back of his head for good measure.

Meanwhile in Berlin, Goering in whom Hitler had invested executive power for the whole of Germany, adopted a procedure similar to that of Hitler's to carry out the purge. He went about the business in an even more ferocious manner than did his Führer. He was determined to take the opportunity to settle old scores with personal enemies as well as S.A. leaders. Himmler and Heydrich had prepared their own black list to which Goering added his own. Schleicher, former Reichschancellor, and his wife were shot dead in their home, as was the daughter of Cavalry General Von Hemmings who happened to be present.

Karl Ernst, waiting at Bremen to sail on a holiday cruise, was dragged back to Berlin. He had been the leader of the incendiaries ordered by the Nazis to fire the Reichstag and had, too often, boasted

German police in action. *Right,* a round-up at the Communist headquarters in Berlin in 1931. *Far right,* a woman is arrested.

about it. The purge presented the ideal opportunity to do away with him and ten other survivors of the band of incendiaries who had become a liability.

Firing squads were kept busy in the Lichterfelde Barracks in Berlin as prisoners were rounded up by the S.S. and Gestapo. Other small groups of picked S.S. and Gestapo killers carried out 'seek and destroy' raids throughout Northern Germany. Gregor Strasser, who had played a big part in the organisation of the Nazi Party but who had fallen foul of Goering and Goebbels, had quit the Party at the end of 1932 to join the pharmaceutical firm of Schering-Kahlbaum. His brother Otto had fled to Austria where he denounced Hitler and formed the anti-Hitler Black Front. To Heydrich was given the task of routing out Gregor and he went about his task with relish. Gregor was arrested and taken to Columbiahaus, a Gestapo prison. He was later removed to a cell of his own where he was badly beaten, shot and left bleeding, unattended, groaning and moaning for an hour while his life ebbed away. Heydrich expressed great satisfaction at the manner of Strasser's death, but Hitler was told that Strasser had committed suicide.

Two Gestapo agents called at the Reich chancellery and shot dead Vice-Chancellor Papen's private secretary, Oberregieningsrat Bose. Director Klausenir, head of Catholic Action, was killed at the Ministry of Transport. General Von Bredow was gunned down by an execution squad. Otto Von Kahn who, as head of the Bavarian Government had been responsible for the launching of the 1923 putsch, was found dead in a wood. Beck, leader of the Catholic students; Captain Erhardt, former Chief of the notorious Freikorps; Gehrt, the flying ace who had been awarded a 'Blue Max' in World War One; Gleiwitz, Chief of Police of Ramshorn; Shrägmuller, Magdeburg police chief; all died on that satanic Saturday murder spree. Others killed included Sander, Voss and Beulitz, members of Karl Ernst's staff. Glaser, the lawyer,

Goebbels, 'the Mouth', lays it on thick to German youth in 1935.

who had brushed with the Nazi jurist Franck, and who had had the temerity to plead against newspapers of the Nazi Party, was cut down in front of his own home. Pröbst, a Düsseldorf youth leader, was shot as he attempted to escape arrest and former Hitler supporter Professor Stempfle, a militant Catholic, was also shot down. Other victims were Laemmermann, head of the Saxony Hitler Youth, and Schmidt, a music critic mistaken for a doctor of the same name. Private vengeance accounted for many more deaths.

In some areas Goering had ordered courts martial for some prisoners, but these hearings were nominal and lasted but a few minutes. With the connivance of the Reichswehr the prisoners were then executed by Heydrich's S.S. firing squads. Whatever the semblance of legality contrived by Goering in the carrying out of the purge the result was invariably death for the victims.

When Hitler arrived by plane in Berlin on the evening of 30 June, Goering and Himmler greeted him and announced with satisfaction the thorough manner in which they had played their part in the great purge. On the afternoon of 1 July the shootings were halted. For a while the bloodbath was over. The estimate of the number of people murdered in the 'Night of the Long Knives' has been variously estimated as between five and seven thousand. Hundreds of prisoners were kept in jail and others were bundled off to the new concentration camps where many died. There were hundreds of men who went in fear of their lives as Hitler's iron grip closed inexorably tighter round the throat of Germany. The monster that the Frankensteins of the Reichswehr and the German industrialists had created between them was in control and nothing could stop his horrific rampage throughout Germany and across Europe.

A month later, on 2 August, Hindenburg died. The day before, even as the old man was fading fast, Hitler, with indecent haste, promulgated the law which gave him the combined functions of Chancellor and President of the Reich. The Reichswehr took the oath of allegiance to Adolf Hitler. On 19 August a rigged plebiscite was conducted to confirm Hitler's new functions, but rigging was hardly necessary. The vast majority of the German people were hopelessly under the spell of their new master. They would follow him to destruction.

Propaganda in Germany, 1933: 'Hitler's fight is for the peace of the world.'

Right, little Nazis due to grow into big Nazis. *Far right,* Hitler, Frick and Roehm, all pals together in 1931.

Sylvia Pankhurst speaks out against the Nazis, 1935.

The bore war

THE WAR BEGAN WITH A FANFARE AND A FLOURISH AND almost immediately, as far as we at home were concerned, the excitement subsided. Then came months of boredom due to black-out of the streets, preposterous snippets of useless information instead of hard news in the media, and none of the heavy air raids we had been expecting. The main effect of all this was for the public to become frustrated and impatient. This period of boredom became known as the 'Sitzkrieg'. The war could drag on for years and years in this dreary way if no action were taken. The people wanted to get on with it and get it over. What was Hitler up to? Why was there no fighting in France? Would there be another Munich after all?

Of course, the Royal Navy and the Merchant Marine were in the war up to their necks, but what was the army doing? And what sort of joke was it for the R.A.F. to risk the lives of men and the loss of aero-planes to fly over Germany to drop useless leaflets? Newspapers having to rely on official communiques of a few laconic lines that told nothing, had to puff out what little news thay did manage to get hold of and serve it up with what we used to call a lot of 'guff'. Military experts who had never been right before and eminent commentators churned out their prognostications which hardly anybody took notice of, and which for the most part, turned out to be wildly wide of the mark.

I had been in the army for months before I even met a soldier who was or had been with the B.E.F. in France. Even the cadre which formed our battalion came straight from Malta. I was stationed near a village not far from Aylesbury, not far down the line from home, when one evening in town, I met a 'real' soldier in a pub. He had been on Christmas leave from France and was returning the next day. He was in the Ox and Bucks Light Infantry and he told me that he should have gone back the previous week but he said that leave was hard to come by and if the fighting ever started, which he was not so sure it would anyway, it would be unlikely that there would be any furlough going, so he might as well take a bit extra now. I asked him why not, in that case, take another week. 'Look, chum,' he said, 'if you're ever kept hanging about and there's nothing on – I mean like you're doing

A familiar sight in 1939 –
London's barrage balloons.

gash guards on a store of pickaxe handles or you're on white-washing coal stores, or put on fetching and carrying for snotty officers' snotty wives – and you asks for 'leaf' and gets a blast instead, you ups and takes it. Mind you, don't wear 'civvies' and always make sure you poodles off back under your own steam. That shows you never had any intention of deserting. You'll only get jankers or local nick, most like, when you get back. It won't be much and in my opinion it's worth it. The most you can get is a firing squad, anyway. Ha! Ha!'

That 'squaddy' was a man after my own heart. He gave me good advice and I made use of it on many occasions, even when I was stationed further afield. He told me that he and two mates were billeted with a French family in a village whose name he was not allowed to divulge and which he could not pronounce anyway. He said that nobody was happy about the billeting arrangements. The Frenchman told him that he reckoned the Germans would pay double what the British paid for billets and when the corporal said he wished him luck if the Germans came, the Frenchman had said something in French that sounded not nice and the corporal had answered in English which definitely was not nice and no mistake.

The soldier from France told me that he had seen no fighting and he was thankful for that, but he had seen a German plane shot down and two dead cows in a field. He said marching made his feet sore and army food was rotten. He wished the war was over, that Hitler was dead, that his R.S.M. got his balls shot off, that he would get his ticket, that he could get back into civvies and that he never had to wear khaki again as it made him itch. He was a likely lad and without a doubt a good soldier. I hope he survived the war.

World War Two started with the German attack on Poland on 1 September 1939. An article in a British magazine said:

If you want a symbol of Poland in arms you will find it not in speeding aircraft, marching masses of infantry, rumbling tanks and mechanised artillery, but in a trooper of the national cavalry. Alert, swift-moving, ready for every eventuality, quick to seize every change in a changing situation – such is the man and the men on whom Poland depends in her hour of supreme crisis . . . Today, as always in the past, Poland's cavalry is the backbone of her army . . . Poland's cavalry, equipped with sword, lance and machine-guns, is said by some best qualified to know to be the best in Europe.

Undaunted by this information, the Germans smashed into Poland with tanks and aircraft. Myths of Polish military prowess and invincible cavalry disappeared in battle smoke. In a few weeks Poland was pulverised. Soon the Poles would be glad to eat their cavalry horses.

News of propaganda leaflets dropped over Germany soon after the

A Hampden medium bomber. This aircraft saw a lot of service from the outbreak of war but without a lot of success.

Headgear to be worn instead of a steel helmet during leaflet raids, perhaps.

outbreak of war was received with incredulity by the majority of the public. The press stated that nothing in the opening stages of the war had been more finely conceived or executed than the leaflet raids made over Germany by the R.A.F. It appeared that in the first week of war, Bomber Command had flown over a wide area of northern and western Germany, including the Ruhr, hazarding men and planes to drop in the first three raids alone, over twenty-five tons of leaflets – while the Poles were being pounded by German bombs. Perhaps the leaflets might have had some effect if they had been dropped in bundles weighing one ton each. They might have damaged a roof or two or even killed some of the enemy. As it was, the pamphlets drifting gently to earth to be picked up by curious Germans for souvenirs, could have had no impact at all. If the Germans had any sense of humour the message contained in the leaflets might have made them laugh. But in Britain it was reported that the pamphlets so annoyed the Nazi authorities that it was said they would have preferred the dropping of bombs.

On 4 September 1939 had come the first French war communique. It stated that operations had begun by 'the whole land, air and sea forces', and later that night it was added that contacts had been progressively made on the front and that aerial forces were proceeding with the necessary reconnaissance. That first communique was a mine of information compared to some subsequent communiques, and the press contrived to read between the lines, make guesses, educated and uneducated, add a few trimmings here and there in order to make 'big 'uns' out of 'little 'uns'.

Somehow the press was able to deduce that some ten days after the start of the campaign, if that is what it could be called, the French had advanced into German territory between the Maginot and Siegfried lines and were in contact with the outer works of the advanced positions of the Siegfried line. In the process all German civilians had evacuated

135

French anti-aircraft guns in action.

The Maginot memorial at Fort Souville, France.

136

the territory and the German army was 'for it'. The fact was that the biggest French city in the zone, Strasbourg, was completely denuded of its civilians – but that, of course, was for strategic reasons.

It was reported that eight giant French tanks, each weighing seventy tons, had made the advance toward the German lines, compelling the enemy to withdraw and blow up the railway line 'in their efforts to stem the advance of the monstrous engines of war'. How the blowing up of a railway line could halt advancing tanks was not stated, nor was it stated, naturally enough, that the French had no more than a dozen of these tanks. Photographs of these monsters were taken at every conceivable angle for propaganda purposes and appeared in newspapers and periodicals all over the world. It might have impressed some people but certainly not the Germans who were better informed about their opposition.

It was reported that the noise of battle along the western front could be heard far away in the streets of Luxembourg and that it was 'obvious that the struggle was developing an unprecedented intensity'. It was not, however, obvious to anybody in the sector where the mighty battle was supposed to be taking place. By the following week, when the French communiques had become more and more laconic, many pressmen were beginning to jibe, blaming official censorship for lack of information. Others hinted that French tactics were wearing down the Germans, that French artillery was plastering the German back areas, that the French inexorable forward movement was giving the enemy the jitters. It was said that Allied aerial reconnaissance above the German lines caused the enemy to cringe in air raid shelters and waste petrol searching for raiders, that by provoking artillery duels the French were forcing the Germans to waste ammunition. It was implied that, whereas the French could afford to waste war material, the Germans could not. All this guff fooled few but it did help fill newspaper columns. Perhaps it made the French and British public cynical, but it made the armed services laugh and that did some good.

A week or so later it was reported in the press that the French guns had suddenly blazed into activity and that French infantry were pushing forward, bringing up their guns and beating off German counter-attacks. The British public was puzzled. What was going on that they did not know about? Something big, for sure. But there were more reports that British airmen continued to rain down deadly leaflets on the heads of the enemy in northern and western Germany.

Just when the folk at home were beginning to think that the fireworks on the western front had fizzled out and were not much to write about, there came news that on the morning of 16 October the Germans east of Moselle near the Luxembourg border had put down a heavy bombardment and, under the cover of a box barrage, had attacked on a front of four miles. It was reported that the enemy used six divisions in the attacks and that the Germans had occupied the heights of Schneeburg. A further communique announced that the Germans had launched a second attack east of the Saar on a front of twenty miles, 'and,' said the French, 'our light troops fell back, fighting in accordance with their mission, but our fire held up the enemy at the prearranged line'.

So just when it was beginning to look as though the war was 'hotting up', it seemed that the French were back at square one and all was quiet on the western front. In the uneasy atmosphere that followed the brief flurry, commentators and experts were quick on the job again, filling in the news gaps. By now the defeated Polish army, which only a few weeks before they had described as formidable, was written off, rightly enough, as badly equipped and old fashioned with an air force of antiquated aeroplanes that could never have hoped to hold off the German attack. A German blitzkrieg could not, of course, succeed against the well equipped modern armies of France and Britain. It was pointed out that the French had driven the Germans from one of the richest industrial areas in the world, a region which was the very life blood of the enemy's armament supplies. The process of the slow French advance toward the Siegfried line was called 'nibbling' by the press. So while the French mice were nervously nibbling, the German alleycat was waiting to pounce.

The war of words continued unabated. The Maginot line was impregnable, or nearly so, and the garrison was dry, comfortable and secure, whereas the Siegfried line was another kettle of fish. It was poorly constructed and there the garrison lived in appalling conditions. The unfortunate Germans were racked with rheumatism, fever and colds because of the damp, were suffering from angina and were complaining bitterly of the lack of aspirin, quinine and warm underclothing. It was surprising then that the Allies, bursting with health, should not have descended there and then on these wretched invalids.

The Germans were hungry. Ellen Wilkinson M.P. wrote that an enemy breakfast consisted of malt coffee, bread, margarine and jam. For dinner and supper the Germans had to make do with potatoes, 'cooked in every conceivable way', supplemented by red cabbage, sauerkraut, stewed vegatables or an omelette of egg substitute. Meat and fish appeared once a day. From the quantities given, these could only be regarded as 'flavourings'. Whether this was true or not, most British soldiers fared a good deal worse most of the time and, after a while, the British public not much better. In fact, towards the end of October people at home were beginning to ask why was the rationing

of food and petrol necessary? And the glib answer to that was that many men in the army were eating more than they had done as civilians. If that was the case, most men in the army must have been near starvation before the war. Also it was asserted that rationing ensured a fair distribution among rich and poor alike. Perhaps in

The Bren gun, standard automatic weapon of 1939, mounted on fixed lines.

Preparing for war – a Cardon light tank which was superseded by the famous Bren carrier.

139

theory, but everyone soon got to know that money could buy just about anything on the black market. Incidentally, at the same time, it was reported that, 'Mr Anthony Eden sat down to an eight course lunch when he visited the Maginot line'. While Germany claimed that she was 'starving Britain and France', Mr Eden, with a French general, was enjoying hare with onions and wine, creamed mushrooms and Neapolitan ice. It was always all right for some. In one periodical under the headline, 'None but the best for the British army', it was stated that the diet of the British troops was a generous one, and that the daily ration for a soldier was: bread, 16 oz.; potatoes, 12 oz.; meat, 14 oz.; bacon, 3 oz.; vegetable, 8 oz.; cheese, 1 oz. There were ample allowances of butter, margarine, tea, milk, rice, salt, pepper and mustard. Also there were regular issues of tinned herrings and tinned salmon, cigarettes and matches. Civilians read this, believed it and were envious.

Some news items were so puerile it is doubtful if anybody could have taken them seriously. In the middle of October, war news included such snippets as, 'Gas masks for children will soon be available in pastel shades. This, it is thought, will make them less repellent to their wearers'. A few weeks later delighted parents learned that, 'Special Mickey Mouse and Donald Duck gas masks in various colours and having separate eyepieces and a little nose are being made for small children'. Did the Disney organisation get royalties? It was also comforting to read that most zoo animals were immune to tear gas, though monkeys might be slightly affected.

There was an eye witness account by a Berlin correspondent of a daily newspaper, just returned to England, who had observed the Germans marching off on 28 August to invade Poland. He wrote:

I watched columns of older reservists march to the trains that were to carry them to points near the Polish border. There was no flag waving, no military bands. The men shambled along dejectedly. Bald heads were seen all along the line and no one within the ranks was without greying hair. One man in five seemed to have snow white hair.

It was reported that Germans stationed in conquered Poland were very depressed and were buying civilian clothing preparatory to deserting and that German authorities had had barbed wire erected all along the frontier to prevent mass desertion by their soldiers. Rather inconsistent with this was another report which stated that German soldiers, begging for food over the Dutch frontier, had been given it with the remark, 'Eat, but may Hitler starve'. Did the German soldiers touch their forelocks and say, 'Thank 'e kindly, Sir'?

Another news item was about a New York family who had tried living on Nazi wartime rations and became in a week, 'morose, irritable and discontented'. It was not stated how the British scale of rations would have affected the same New York family.

On 14 November a British destroyer struck a mine. The survivors must have been speechless at the reports of the sinking in the newspapers. An eyewitness was stated to have said, 'I shall never forget the courage of those men. They were splashing around in the oily water singing "Even Hitler had a Mother".' This was a song from Herbert Farjeon's *Little Revue* at the Little Theatre which started:

> *Even Hitler had a mother,*
> *Even Hitler had a ma;*
> *Although he may suffer for his sins,*
> *At least, thank God, he wasn't twins.*

If someone had asked the eyewitness what the shipwrecked sailors had sung for an encore, he would, no doubt, have thought of something.

It was thought that the British would be heartened by the news that German shoemakers converted summer shoes into winter shoes by applying strong soles and heels, and that German schoolchildren aided

Nazi propaganda by writing persuasive letters to French children, but did not say whether the Germans wrote in French or the French children read German, nor how the letters were delivered. It was also reported that German children were getting into trouble because they had discovered that by blowing down the spout of a water can, they could imitate an air raid siren. Did the British really imagine a German child blowing feebly into a water can could send tough Germans scurrying into their air raid shelters?

Once again, the British heard that the percentage of sick men from the Siegfried line was causing anxiety to the German authorities.

The British public was reminded every so often about the impregnability of the Maginot line as some measure of the debt which free nations owed France, and that German U-boats were fighting a dirty war. One periodical stated in early December that in the last few weeks the German U-boats, having largely abandoned the gun for the torpedo, had descended from the torpedo to the mine and that it was about the lowest form of warfare that could be fought, that it was the warfare of the I.R.A. leaving the bomb in parcel offices of railway stations.

Newspapers gave out the cryptic news early in December that the B.E.F. had gone into action for the first time on 1 December and that they were mainly Midland county regiments who had taken over a sector of the Maginot line. The first British soldier killed in France was Corporal Thomas Priday, who was killed on 9 December whilst leading a patrol.

Newspapers and periodicals commenting on the 'few German reconnaissance raids' on Britain up until December, said the results indicated that the long heralded blitzkrieg, if and when it did come, would not succeed.

A big story was made of a German air raid on the Shetlands on

13 November, when the press claimed that the total result of this devastating raid by a German plane was the death of a rabbit. There were photographs of a bomb crater with the rabbit's body on the edge. It had not been blown to bits. It was announced that Field Marshal Goering, chief of the Nazi Air Force and Grand Master of the Chase, noted for his ability as a huntsman, had been presented with the rabbit that 'his Heinkel plane had bombed to death on the Shetlands on 13 November'. One periodical stated:

The story of how this 'bag', which would cost 1s. 6d. [7½p] retail in England, but which cost the German people about £100,000 in planes and ammunition, was sent to the gallant Nazi sportsman, is being told in the R.A.F. messes in France. After the Nazis had failed to collect their prize, it was considered unsportsmanlike by a certain squadron of the R.A.F. not to do something about it. The little rabbit was accordingly transferred from its most remote Shetland Isle to the cockpit of an R.A.F. plane about to set off on a reconnaissance flight over Germany. The rabbit was duly dropped in the Reich addressed to Field Marshal Goering. Attached to its tail was a message of regret that the 'bag' was so small after the most magnificently organised shoot in history. 'But,' said the message, 'it is being said round Shetland way that rabbits are very much on the alert this year'.

In the 'Daily Telegraph' there was a suggestion that the popular song success of the moment should now read:

Run rabbit, run rabbit, run, run, run;
Don't give the bombers their fun, fun, fun.
They'll get by without their rabbit pie;
Run rabbit, run from the Hun, Hun, Hun.

Cynical servicemen alleged that Goering had replied to the alleged R.A.F. message by ordering his air force to drop twelve buckets of bullshit over England. If that was so it probably went unnoticed; there was already too much of it about.

The newpapers dished up this item for the first Christmas of the war:

Christmas will be kept up in the real British way under far better conditions than in 1914. An idea of what sort of Christmas it is to be for the men can be gathered from the typical menu for the R.A.F. The dinner includes creme of tomato soup; fried fillet of sole and lemon; roast turkey, roast pork and apple sauce, roast potatoes and cauliflower; Christmas pudding and brandy sauce'.

The real war was soon to start.